Designing an HerbGarden

Beth Hanson

EDITOR

Janet Marinelli
SERIES EDITOR

Sigrun Wolff Saphire
SENIOR EDITOR

Kerry Barringer
SCIENCE EDITOR

Leah Kalotay
ART DIRECTOR

Joni Blackburn
COPY EDITOR

Steven Clemants
VICE-PRESIDENT,
SCIENCE &
PUBLICATIONS

Judith D. Zuk
PRESIDENT

Elizabeth Scholtz
DIRECTOR
EMERITUS

Handbook #179

Copyright © 2004 by Brooklyn Botanic Garden, Inc.

All-Region Guides, formerly *21st-Century Gardening
Series,* are published three times a year at
1000 Washington Ave., Brooklyn, NY 11225.

Subscription included in Brooklyn Botanic Garden
subscriber membership dues ($35 per year;
$45 outside the United States).

ISBN # 1-889538-63-9

Printed by Science Press, a division of the Mack
Printing Group. Printed on recycled paper.

**Above: At the Enfield Shaker Museum, large rectangular beds are used to keep a profusion of herbs
well organized and easily accessible. Cover: A lavender-edged path sends a warm welcome.**

Designing an Herb Garden

A Short History of Herb Garden Design

Deirdre Larkin

Whatever their design or intent, herb gardens are defined not by their organization but by the plants grown in them. If an herb is a plant with a use as a seasoning, fragrance, dye, fiber, or medicine, then an herb garden is a garden of useful plants. But don't be surprised to find species that have never had any practical application alongside the useful plants in today's ornamental herb gardens—some plants are simply too appealing to be excluded on purely technical grounds. Besides, our habit of dividing plants into the "useful" and the "ornamental" is relatively new. In medieval Europe virtually all plants were assumed to have some medicinal value. In the Renaissance, medicine, botany, and horticulture began to diverge, but they were slow to part ways and did not really separate for several centuries.

Garden layouts that date back to medieval and Renaissance Europe continue to strongly influence modern herb gardeners. Though we know very little about the dooryard gardens of simpler households—the ancestors of informal cottage herb gardens, in which useful plants were grown close to hand in unstructured plantings— we do have some knowledge about the structured gardens of the great medieval monasteries and royal palaces.

The earliest visual representation of a formal garden to survive the Middle Ages, found on the St. Gall plan, dates to the ninth century. This master plan for an ideal

Practical as well as ornamental, formal herb gardens laid out in simple beds date back to medieval Europe and continue to be popular today, as this contemporary take on a 12th-century garden attests.

Benedictine monastery, which was never built as planned, includes a large, rectangular kitchen garden with 18 beds of vegetables and potherbs and a smaller square garden with 16 beds of medicinal herbs. This small healing garden is located next to the doctor's house and near the infirmary. Both gardens are walled and are laid out in two parallel rows of rectangular raised beds, each bed devoted to a single species.

This basic, utilitarian design is typical not only of monastic but of other medieval gardens as well. Enclosed gardens of rural manors and townhouses are depicted in a number of 15th-century illuminations in Piero de Crescenzi's popular treatise on horticulture and agriculture, *Liber Ruralia Commodorum* (On the Management of Country Estates). They too are made up of a number of small square or rectangular beds arranged in a simple grid pattern. The paths between the beds allow easy access to the plots.

This type of plan is still used today in our own vegetable gardens and is ideal for herb gardens, making it easy to cultivate and harvest the herbs and rotate short-lived crops of salad herbs and annuals. It is both functional in form and visually pleasing in its simplicity and neatness.

Not all medieval gardens were purely utilitarian. Unlike the gardens of the St. Gall plan, the small, private pleasure garden or "herber" was a place of beauty and refreshment rather than a home for useful plants. In the 13th century, Albertus Magnus gave directions for laying out an herber, recommending that the lawn at the center of the garden be surrounded by borders of sweet-smelling herbs such as rue, basil, and sage. These early pleasure gardens emphasized elements we still associate with our own ornamental herb gardens: enclosure, intimacy, and fragrance.

Created as teaching gardens by university faculties of medicine, the burgeoning botanical gardens of the Renaissance favored the narrow, rectangular beds of the medieval type. In the Chelsea Physic Garden in London, founded by the London Society of Apothecaries in the 17th century, the beds still in use today are in the medieval style.

The Renaissance also gave rise to the collector's garden, in which botanists organized their plants according to scientific principles and plantsmen exhibited horticultural rarities. Though many new plants were grown, the gardens themselves remained geometric in form and fairly simple in their organization, and their descent from the gardens of the Middle Ages is very clear.

As in the Middle Ages, formal gardens of the Renaissance favored all sorts of enclosures—brick, stone, wattle fencing, or hedges—to keep out animals and intruders.

Large formal herb gardens were the domain of monasteries, manor houses, and palaces. Simpler households grew useful plants in unstructured dooryard plantings, where they would be close at hand when needed for cooking and other purposes.

Throughout the 17th century, the practice of enclosing household gardens persisted. Even today, kitchen gardens are often enclosed for practical reasons (rabbits and deer are with us yet).

During the Renaissance, garden makers went beyond the basic forms of the medieval garden, organizing the squares and rectangles into more complex patterns. The knot, with its decorative interlacing bands of clipped herbs, became a feature of the pleasure garden. A geometric design within a square, rectangle, or circle was drawn on the ground, and each figure in the pattern was planted out with a single herb, closely clipped to maintain the design. Gardeners often filled in the spaces between the clipped outlines with colored sand or gravel. Elizabethan gardeners used lavender, germander, and santolina to lay out their knots. Boxwood became the plant of choice by the 17th century and is still the most popular today. Many patterns for these designs survive, and the knot lives on as the most elaborate and ambitious type of formal herb garden.

In the 18th and 19th centuries, farmers and householders usually mixed vegetables,

Productive gardens remained medieval in character for many centuries, as this recreation of a colonial garden shows. The idea of dividing plants into the "useful" and the "ornamental" is a relatively new development that started in the Renaissance as medicine, botany, and horticulture began to diverge.

herbs, fruits, and flowers in a single garden. Like the household gardens of the 16th and 17th centuries, utilitarian gardens were essentially medieval in character.

Late in the 19th century, in reaction to Victorian bedding schemes of newly imported exotic plants from around the globe, English ornamental gardeners became interested in "old-fashioned" plants and gardens. This trend had its counterpart in the Colonial Revival movement in the United States, in which writers such as Alice Morse Earle extolled the charms of the 18th-century American garden, with its box-bordered beds and traditional cottage-garden herbs and flowers.

In the first half of the 20th century, scholars like Agnes Arber reclaimed the botanical legacy of the Renaissance, and in the 1920s and '30s, Eleanor Sinclair Rohde helped popularize old English herbals, publishing many books and articles and designing herb gardens based on medieval and Tudor patterns.

In 1931, after years of study and experiment, Maude Grieve published her *Modern Herbal*, the first comprehensive encyclopedia of herbs published in English since the 17th century. This classic of herbal literature contains historical and horticultural information on hundreds of herbs, describing their chemical properties and medicinal and industrial uses. In 1933, American gardeners founded the Herb Society of America to promote the knowledge and appreciation of herbs. Its members have created and maintained many public and private herb gardens.

In the late 1940s Vita Sackville-West relaid and extended a small plot of herbs at her Elizabethan manor in Kent, England, creating the famous formal herb garden at Sissinghurst. Though Sackville-West used historical elements in her quartered design, its emphasis on color and texture makes it an outstanding and influential example of the modern ornamental herb garden.

Lately gardeners have become increasingly interested in the ornamental qualities of the herb garden. In the last 20 years the plant list has greatly expanded as new color forms and cultivars of herbs long grown for their usefulness have been developed. Many foliage plants that are considered herblike in texture, form, or fragrance are now admitted to the herb garden. Experiments with color in the herb garden have also inspired the inclusion of many purely ornamental flowering plants. At the same time, plants appreciated for their medicinal or other uses continue to find new homes among more traditional garden herbs.

This trend may be the logical outcome of the ornamental herb garden's evolution as a distinct garden type, but our definition of herb garden has become a little vague—how can we distinguish an herb garden with a mixture of perennials and ornamental annuals from a perennial garden or a mixed border that includes a large number of herbs? Perhaps the proportion of useful herbs to ornamentals doesn't matter. The important thing is to keep growing herbs and create our own place in a long tradition.

An Easy Formal Herb Garden

Donna Gerbosi-DiFulvio

Like many gardeners, I used to find formal herb gardens a little intimidating. I had always admired parterres and intricately woven herbal knots but was put off by the weekly—if not daily—trimming they require. Who has that kind of time? Naturalistic settings always seemed much more my style.

Unwisely, I forgot to take into consideration three crucial points: I generally avoid weeding until things get out of hand; I'm a shameless plant collector; and I live in a small suburban home with a formal, red-brick exterior.

It eventually occurred to me that my property looked constantly, well, messy. I took a good hard look at my chaotic flower beds, their original design ruined by my acquisitive nature, and completely rethought my garden. I created a separate small, formal space with a limited color scheme and high-impact, low-maintenance herbs. It turned out to be just what I needed: I'm still willing to adopt plants for other spots in the garden, but I truly relish having one area that's always orderly.

My formal garden design offers the ease I'd been searching for as well as surprising flexibility. With the four quadrants of the garden planted in curved rows, I can readily rotate herbs in and out to build on past successes or eliminate failures. I can also try new combinations without compromising the inherent garden scheme. By choosing

Continued on page 14

First developed during the Renaissance, herb gardens featuring plants in complex geometric patterns, such as this 17th-century example at Bodysgallen in Wales, require constant grooming.

A Formal Herb Garden

Achieving the beauty and repose of a simple formal design is straightforward. Select a basic geometric shape such as a circle or square and divide it into equal parts. Then plant each section with the same combination of herbs, or choose plants that complement each other.

Structure is the most important part of any formal garden. In the design I'm suggesting, the structure is clearly established by four elements: a germander (*Teucrium chamaedrys*) hedge forming the perimeter of the garden; brick pathways edging the beds and giving access to the garden; a garden seat inviting quiet reflection; and a large central planter occupied by a golden bay tree (*Laurus nobilis* 'Aurea') serving as a focal point and vertical accent. (In cooler climates, the planter can move indoors for the winter.)

In your own garden, you're free to modify this theme to your liking. You could make paths of turf, creeping chamomile (*Chamaemelum nobile*), or pea gravel raked in a decorative pattern. Your focal point might be a birdhouse, sundial, or tiered fountain. The entire space could be enclosed by high walls. If you're ambitious, you might create an intricate labyrinth in which to meander among soothing scented herbs.

Design Tips

- Limit plant colors in a formal garden to achieve the desired cohesive look. This design features a predominantly green, gold, and burgundy color scheme. For an entirely different look, substitute silver and blue plants or those with coral, deep maroon, and dark green foliage.

- To create interest, place plants with contrasting habits and leaf textures in the same bed. To unify and balance the garden without being redundant, use herbs with similar forms and textures in the different beds.

- Place herbs with similar sun and moisture requirements together in the separate beds to keep plants healthy and simplify maintenance.

Plants Featured in This Garden

1 *Alchemilla alpina*, mountain lady's mantle

2 *Allium senescens* subsp. *montanum*, mountain chives

3 *Laurus nobilis* 'Aurea', golden bay

4 *Ocimum* × 'African Blue', 'African Blue' basil

5 *Ocimum basilicum* 'Mimimum', 'Minimum' Greek bush basil

6 *Origanum vulgare* 'Aureum', golden oregano

7 *Pelargonium* 'Charity', 'Charity' scented geranium

8 *Pelargonium* 'Poquito', 'Poquito' scented geranium

9 *Petroselinum crispum* var. *crispum*, curly parsley

10 *Rosmarinus officinalis* 'Gorizia', 'Gorizia' rosemary

11 *Rumex sanguineus*, bloody sorrel

12 *Ruta graveolens*, rue

13 *Sanguisorba minor*, salad burnet

14 *Satureja hortensis*, summer savory

15 *Teucrium chamaedrys*, germander

16 *Thymus herba-barona*, caraway thyme

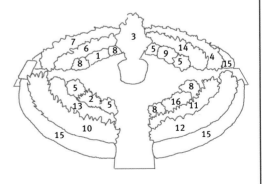

Simple formal gardens with symmetrically laid-out square or rectangular beds are far from a maintenance nightmare. Useful for herbs as well as vegetables, these time-honored designs allow easy access to all plants, making plant care and harvest a breeze.

appropriately sized plants that respect their boundaries and picking others that form tight clusters that help control weeds, I have more time to devote to other, more demanding garden beds—or just unwind with a glass of good wine.

Picking Plants for a Formal Garden

To maintain a cohesive look, limit plant colors in a formal garden. The design on page 12 features a predominately green, gold, and burgundy theme. A rich, dark purple-red holds the eye; bright gold illuminates choice spots; and varying shades of green foliage temper the contrasts and tie everything together.

As you choose herbs for your garden, also consider leaf size and shape, plant habit, bloom time, and flower and stem color. Select herbs that relate to others in a variety of ways. I positioned summer savory (*Satureja hortensis*), a fine-needled herb, between the furled green leaves of curly parsley (*Petroselinum crispum* var. *crispum*) and the bold, purple-backed and -veined 'African Blue' basil (*Ocimum* × 'African Blue'). The three plants vary in foliage color and shape, providing contrast. I put caraway thyme (*Thymus herba-barona*), summer savory, and robust rosemary 'Gorizia' (*Rosmarinus officinalis* 'Gorizia')—which all have similar leaf forms and colors—in different beds. Planted together they might look somewhat boring, but in different beds, they help unify the garden.

Also remember that plants evolve throughout the growing season and complement each other in different ways from spring to fall. The young foliage of salad burnet (*Sanguisorba minor*), for example, unfurls a light yellow-green and matures to darker green. And as they start to flower, the plants add a new color dimension to the garden. Spread around the garden, mountain chives (*Allium senescens* subsp. *montanum*), salad burnet, caraway thyme, and germander provide rose-colored accents when they are in bloom. The dainty pale flowers of summer savory and Greek bush basil (*Ocimum basilicum* 'Minimum') offset the vivid leaves and purple flowers of African blue basil, which blooms nonstop until frost. The gold foliage of scented *Pelargonium* 'Charity', variegated golden sage (*Salvia officinalis* 'Icterina'), golden bay, and golden oregano (*Origanum vulgare* 'Aureum') accent the gold flowers of mountain lady's mantle (*Alchemilla alpina*) and rue (*Ruta graveolens*).

Choose herbs that complement not only their immediate neighbors but also those in the next bed or across the path. Both caraway thyme and mountain lady's mantle, for example, have creeping habits, and I situated them across the garden from each other. Likewise, mountain chives and curly parsley, which both have an upright growth habit, are opposite each other. Gardeners generally site short plants in the front of a bed, medium ones in the middle, and tall herbs in the back. But as my formal garden has a circular center path, I've placed the shorter herbs right by the path, and I also keep the germander edging clipped to a uniform, low height so it doesn't impede the view from the outer edges.

In this garden, the four quadrants tell their own color story, with burgundy to dark green giving way to sunny gold and green. Many of the herbs planted here are available in other hues; you can achieve an entirely different look by substituting silver and blue plants, or those with coral, deep maroon and dark green foliage, for those in my garden.

Originally used to keep hungry animals and other intruders at bay, enclosures such as walls and fences help create intimate garden spaces.

Herbs for an Easy Formal Garden

Alchemilla alpina
Mountain Lady's Mantle

Historically used to treat female disorders, mountain lady's mantle is an irresistibly diminutive version of the much larger *Alchemilla mollis*. It can grow to 6 inches high and spread by stolons to 18 inches across. Its small green foliage is deeply cut into five to seven lobes, each tip lightly toothed and the entire leaf edged and backed by fine, silvery hairs. The leaves cradle sparkling pearls of dew; this liquid was once thought to have magical powers. Tiny clusters of yellow-green flowers appear in late spring.

Growing Tips Sow seed in moist, well-drained soil in early spring; divide established plants in spring or fall. A herbaceous mat-forming perennial, mountain lady's mantle grows well in full sun but should be offered some shade in hotter climates. Hardy in Zones 3 to 8.

Cultivars and Related Species *Alchemilla conjuncta*, a much taller clumping species, has blue-green foliage bearing seven to nine lobes and is often mistaken for the much smaller *A. alpina*. *A. mollis* is a clump-forming species with larger, less incised foliage that grows to 24 inches high and spreads to 30 inches wide.

Companion Plants Lady's mantle is delightful anywhere you can admire its refined nature. Site in semishade with shiny European ginger (*Asarum europaeum*) or North American native wild ginger (*Asarum canadense*, page 78) and the dark, crinkled leaves of noninvasive bugleweed (*Ajuga pyramidalis* 'Metallica Crispa Purpurea').

Allium senescens subsp. *montanum*
Mountain Chives, German Garlic

Native to mountainous regions of Europe through Asia, the straplike foliage of mountain chives emerges in spring a glossy, shamrock green. The flat, slightly twisted leaves are a mere quarter-inch wide, grow 12 inches long, and emit an onion scent when crushed. The solid, relatively slow-growing clumps are almost impervious to weeds and relatively trouble-free. Rose colored, 1½-inch umbels perch on 12- to 18-inch stems in midsummer and remain attractive a long time. It can be difficult to distinguish the differences between this subspecies of *Allium senescens* and the naturally occurring deviants. Therefore always look for broad, flat, shiny green leaves when buying this plant.

Growing Tips Sow seeds directly in the ground in full sun to partial shade and well-drained soil in spring, or divide clumps in spring or fall. Hardy in Zones 5 to 9.

Alchemilla alpina, **mountain lady's mantle.**

Cultivars and Related Species Silver corkscrew chives (*Allium senescens* subsp. *glaucum*) have short, highly twisted gray foliage, up to six inches high, and soft pink flowers. 'Sterile' chives (*A. schoenoprasum* 'Sterile'), a culinary variety, produce lots of flowers that don't set seeds; they're also super on a kitchen windowsill.

Companion Plants Mountain chives look pristine in a border foreground, naturalized in rock gardens, or as a groundcover. Pair in a cottage garden with the darker magenta flowers of wood betony (*Stachys officinalis*) and dwarf purple coneflower (*Echinacea purpurea* 'Kim's Knee High') along with the softer pinkish-purple flowers of lemon mint (*Monarda citriodora*) and the white flowers of Italian oregano or hardy marjoram (*Origanum × majoricum*).

Allium senescens subsp. *montanum*, **mountain chives.**

Laurus nobilis 'Aurea' Golden Bay

Easily pruned into an elegant standard, golden bay has the regal beauty of Grecian bay (*Laurus nobilis*, page 30), enhanced by foliage that emerges a golden color (further promoted by full sun). Mature plants can reach 50 feet tall and 30 feet wide, but golden bay is slow-growing and does well in a container. Harvest bay leaves as needed to flavor sauces, soups, and stews. A dried bay leaf kept inside the flour canister repels insects. Handle bay with care; it can irritate sensitive skin.

Growing Tips All bays grow slowly when they are young. In the ground, they need a protected location against a south-facing wall and prefer warm, humid summers. Prune to shape, and propagate by removing suckers to use for cuttings. In a container, provide well-drained moist but not wet loamy soil. In areas where bay is not hardy, move the plant inside to overwinter in a cool, sunny location. Repot every two to three years, pruning roots unless transplanting into a larger container. Where it is hardy, bay may freeze to the ground in severe winters, but it rebounds from the roots in spring. Bay is prone to scale and should be inspected often, especially when grown indoors. Remove scale with a soft-bristled brush dipped in either rubbing alcohol or in a very diluted soapy water solution. Hardy in Zones 8 to 10; marginally hardy in Zone 7 (cover plants with a heavy cloth or a box).

Cultivars and Related Species Willow leaf bay (*Laurus nobilis* 'Angustifolia' or 'Salicifolia') has narrow, curvy-edged, light green leaves and is hardier than the species. *Laurus nobilis* 'Undulata' is a shorter shrub with wavy leaves, and 'Saratoga' has very large rounded leaves.

Companion Plants Pair a large golden bay with the spicy, egg-shaped leaves of

Mexican oregano (*Lippia graveolens*) at the entrance to an arbor covered with the purple-green leaves, lavender flowers, and purple-red seedpods of purple hyacinth bean (*Lablab purpureus*, formerly *Dolichos lablab*). Surround bay in a container with low-growing groundcovers such as golden oregano (*Origanum vulgare* subsp. *vulgare* 'Aureum', page 19), or French or English thyme (such as *Thymus vulgaris* 'Broadleaf English', page 60, or 'Narrowleaf French', page 112)—but avoid herbs that need lots of water, since their roots will compete with bay roots. Where hardy, bay makes a regal hedge.

Ocimum basilicum 'Minimum' 'Minimum' Greek Bush Basil

Ocimum × 'African Blue' 'African Blue' Basil

'Minimum' Greek bush basil is a charming tiny-leafed annual that grows into a striking eight-inch medium-green globe that needs little, if any, shaping. The flavorful, deeply fragrant ovate leaves ¼ to ½ inch long can be used as a pasta garnish.

Dainty white blossoms appear in late summer but should be removed to encourage leaf production.

The rapid, continuous growth and flowering of 'African Blue' basil makes this majestic ornamental, which grows to four feet tall, a choice specimen for any large container or ornamental garden, especially when combined with black, silver, or purple plants. The serrated leaves have a reddish-purple tint, most evident on new foliage, as do the stems, leaf backs, and veins. This camphor-scented hybrid is edible but generally not favored for cooking. Dozens of six-inch lavender flower spikes, which don't inhibit further growth, appear from early summer until frost. They are show-stoppers in floral arrangements.

Growing Tips Plant all basil in full sun in well-drained, humus-rich soil. This subtropical herb needs hot weather to be really productive and is quite sensitive to frost. Stem cuttings of 'African Blue' basil root quickly in a glass of water. Sow seeds of Greek bush basil in spring where they are to grow. Basil is a true annual.

Cultivars and Related Species Sweet 'Baja' basil (*Ocimum basilicum* 'Baja') has a hint of cinnamon and is great for baking; *Ocimum* 'Mrs. Burns' Lemon' (page 46) is a superior citrus-scented variety.

Companion Plants Greek bush basil makes a strong sculptural statement when used as an ornamental edging in a formal dwarf herb garden along with furry silver woolly thyme (*Thymus praecox* subsp. *arcticus* 'Lanuginosus'), gray-green dwarf sage (*Salvia officinalis* 'Nana', page 58), prostrate rosemary (*Rosmarinus officinalis* 'Huntington Carpet'), and the tightly curled dark

Ocimum × 'African Blue', 'African Blue' basil.

Origanum vulgare 'Aureum', golden oregano.

green leaves of moss curled parsley (*Petroselinum crispum* 'Afro').

Origanum vulgare 'Aureum'
Golden Oregano

Wow! The glowing chartreuse foliage of golden oregano immediately draws you in. This plant has a mild flavor and is best used ornamentally as a soft, low grower to six inches tall. It'll be glad to oblige anywhere in the garden. Lavender-pink flowers on 30-inch stems appear in summer.

Growing Tips Golden oregano absolutely needs good air circulation and well-drained soil to prevent disease. Full sun promotes the best gold color, but the plant tolerates partial shade. It can become completely green in hot weather or late in the season. It doesn't come true from seed, so propagate it by division. Hardy in Zones 5 to 9.

Cultivars and Related Species *Origanum laevigatum* 'Herrenhausen', page 110, is sweet-scented, with dark green leaves and purple flowers; the ancient hyssop or "ezov" of the Bible is thought to be Syrian oregano (*O. syriacum*), also called "za'atar" in Arabic. It has highly aromatic leaves with an oregano-thyme scent and flavor and looks like a larger version of pot marjoram (*Origanum onites*).

Companion Plants For an electric grouping, plant golden oregano with yellow- and green-splashed ginger mint (*Mentha arvensis* 'Variegata'), shocking-green lime thyme (*Thymus* 'Lime'), and gold- and green-striped spiky yucca (*Yucca filamentosa* 'Golden Sword').

Pelargonium 'Charity'
'Charity' Scented Geranium
Pelargonium 'Poquito'
'Poquito' Scented Geranium

'Charity' scented geranium (not to be confused with the genus *Geranium*) has sturdy, dense, green oak-leaf-shaped foliage with spectacular lime edges and small lavender-colored flowers appearing on one- to three-foot-tall plants. It is beautiful massed in a large container or left to sprawl across the edges of a patio or walkway where it can be frequently caressed, releasing the delicious lemon-rose scent that permeates its leaves. Use these for baking, in beverages, or for scenting sugars.

'Poquito' scented geranium is a terrific bushy little plant that shines when placed front and center in a border or container. Its small, crisp foliage is deeply divided and has purplish-brown midribs. The slightly sticky leaves have a pungent scent. Tiny lavender flowers appear in late summer.

Growing Tips Native to South Africa, scented geraniums are not reliably cold-hardy, but they may overwinter in a pro-tected location to Zone 7. Plant in full sun to partial shade. Take softwood cut-tings in late summer and late winter; they will root easily and make great

houseplants or standards. Scented pelargoniums can be susceptible to rust and other diseases if not provided with good air circulation. Grown indoors, they can be prone to whitefly; treat with sticky traps placed near the plant. Hardy in Zones 9 and 10.

Cultivars and Related Species Most scented pelargoniums have small blossoms, but the flowers of the cultivars 'Clorinda', 'Copthorne', 'Lime', 'Orange', and 'Paton's Unique' are all larger and much showier. 'Mabel Gray' is intensively lemon-scented and has crisp green maple-leaf foliage.

Companion Plants Use *Pelargonium* 'Charity' in the back of a border with licorice-scented and -flavored Mexican tarragon (*Tagetes lucida*, page 70) and flamboyant Mexican sage (*Salvia mexicana* 'Tula'), which has lime-green calyces and royal-blue corollas.

Rumex sanguineus
Bloody Sorrel, Red-Veined Dock

The striking color of bloody sorrel's long, arrowhead-shaped leaves will stop you in your tracks. Medium green foliage is shot through with deep red veining and attached to stems even more incredibly vivid. This hardy perennial, which can reach 12 inches tall, emerges in early spring and produces new foliage all season. Young leaves of bloody sorrel are edible, but the plant is simply too gorgeous to eat. Leave it alone to bask in its own glory and cook with French sorrel (*Rumex scutatus*) instead.

Growing Tips Plant in moist, well-drained, moderately fertile soil in full sun to part shade. Divide this clumping sor-rel every three to four years to revitalize the bed. Remove the green and red flow-

Rumex sanguineus, bloody sorrel.

ers to promote new leaf growth. Young sorrel leaves taste the best; during the hotter months, the leaves may develop a bitter flavor. Hardy in Zones 6 to 8.

Cultivars and Related Species The leaves of variegated sorrel (*Rumex acetosa* 'Rhubarb Pie') emerge in spring a startling coral pink. With the advent of hot weather, they mottle into a coral, cream, and green pattern. Silver buckler's sorrel (*R. scutatus* 'Silver Shield') is a spreading groundcover with small, silver-green leaves.

Companion Plants Bloody sorrel looks snappy with purple sage (*Salvia officinalis* 'Purpurascens') and the mottled, pungent foliage of the holy basil cultivar *Ocimum basilicum* 'Red & Green'.

Ruta graveolens
Rue, Herb of Grace

Centuries ago, artists ingested rue to improve bleary vision, and rue leaves are still used today as a flavoring ingredient in some grappas. Its trilobed leaf tips are reputed to be the inspiration for the suit of clubs in playing cards. The blue-green, waxy-coated foliage is adored by the larvae of black swallowtail butterflies. Small, four-petaled mustard-yellow flowers appear on this two-foot-tall, semievergreen perennial in summer. Some people develop moderate to severe contact dermatitis, similar to poison ivy, after handling rue in sunlight, so wear gloves when working around this herb. Rue is generally not consumed in the United States and Canada and may be toxic to some.

Growing Tips Grow rue in moist but not wet soil. After the first year, cut it back in spring to six inches above the ground to keep the plant bushy. Rue is attractive to whitefly when temperatures soar or when grown indoors. Remove whitefly eggs, larvae, and adults with a sharp

Ruta graveolens, rue.

stream of water directed at the plant, or trap whiteflies with sticky traps placed near the plants. Hardy in Zones 6 to 9.

Cultivars and Related Species *Ruta graveolens* 'Jackman's Blue' has blue-gray leaves; 'Variegata' has a cream variegation; 'Blue Mound' is a compact blue form.

Companion Plants Rue rounds out a soothing palette with long-stemmed, purple-flowering lavandin 'Grosso' (*Lavandula × intermedia* 'Grosso', page 55), the aromatic soft, feathery foliage of 'Powis Castle' wormwood (*Artemisia* 'Powis Castle'), and the crinkled gray-green leaves of clary sage (*Salvia sclarea*).

Sanguisorba minor
Salad Burnet, Burnet

Salad burnet is the frilly ballerina of the herb garden, yet its ethereal appearance belies the underlying hardiness of this evergreen perennial. Golden-green pinnate foliage, with arching stems to

Sanguisorba minor, salad burnet.

spikes three feet tall. The outstanding foliage is edged in creamy white.

Companion Plants Salad burnet's refined nature complements the tiny, yellow-green, grasslike foliage of licorice sweet flag (*Acorus gramineus* 'Licorice') and the soft golden edible flowers of 'Stella d'Oro' daylily (*Hemerocallis* 'Stella d'Oro').

Satureja hortensis
Summer Savory

The German name for savory translates as bean herb, alluding to the herb's reputation as a flavorful digestive aid for gassy vegetables like beans and cabbage. The bright green, narrow foliage has a peppery oregano flavor that many people prefer to winter savory (*Satureja montana,* page 59).

Growing Tips Sow seeds of summer savory in early spring by pressing them into well-drained soil; they need light to germinate. Thin the young plants to six inches apart. Savory tolerates full sun to partial shade but needs a few hours of direct sunlight daily. It can reach 18 inches tall and 12 inches wide and should be repeatedly cut back during the growing season to keep it bushy and productive. Summer savory is a true annual.

Cultivars and Related Species Perennial winter savory (*Satureja montana*) is shrubby with darker green leaves and may be substituted for summer savory in cooking. Tender African lemon savory (*Satureja biflora,* page 37) is native to South Africa and has a distinct lemony note.

18 inches long, unfurls fanlike from a central rosette and matures to a dark green. Rounded leaflets are delicately toothed and have a light cucumber flavor. People who have problems digesting cucumbers often substitute salad burnet leaves in green salads. The leaves also make beautiful garnishes.

Growing Tips Best planted in moist, well-drained soil in full sun, salad burnet will tolerate partial shade, especially in hot climates. In late spring to summer, small round green flowers sporting red-pink stamens appear on spikes. Remove them to encourage leaf production. Situate salad burnet near a path to easily spy its delicate beauty. Hardy in Zones 5 to 10.

Cultivars and Related Species Greater burnet (*Sanguisorba officinalis*) is a taller species with similar looking but much larger leaves. *Sanguisorba officinalis* 'Variegata' has deep burgundy flower

Companion Plants Summer savory is ornamental with the broad, furry, gray-green leaves of lamb's ear (*Stachys byzantina* 'Helene von Stein') and the red flowers of Texas sage (*Salvia coccinea* 'Scarlet').

Teucrium chamaedrys
Germander, Wall Germander

Germander's elegant small, oak-shaped leaves are leathery and aromatic and are used to flavor vermouth. Dark rose tubular flowers appear in midsummer to fall. Germander grows to ten inches tall, and its upright to spreading habit makes it appropriate for a low herbal edging. It makes a good boxwood substitute, especially if you don't care for the latter's odor.

Growing Tips Germander does best in a light, dry soil with a neutral to alkaline pH, in full sun. Cut it back after flowering to encourage new growth. Germander grows well on walls and steep banks. Hardy in Zones 5 to 9.

Cultivars and Related Species *Teucrium chamaedrys* 'Variegatum' has dark green leaves with cream and yellow variegation. *Teucrium × lucidrys*, an upright hybrid with darker green leaves, is suitable for knot gardens; *T. × lucidrys* is taller than *T. chamaedrys* and has glossier, more leathery leaves but is frequently confused with it by nurseries

Companion Plants Germander is very pretty paired with true lavender (*Lavandula angustifolia* 'Hidcote' or 'Royal Velvet', page 55) or grown on a bank or in a rock garden with minor bulbs.

Thymus herba-barona
Caraway Thyme

Covered with dainty, purple-rose flowers in spring, caraway thyme produces a fine-textured, soft mat that creeps along the ground. The deep green needled foliage on foot-long multibranched, arching stems possesses a heady caraway-seed aroma and flavor and is useful for

Thymus herba-barona, caraway thyme.

baking and in meat dishes. This is a solid choice for creating a thyme lawn.

Growing Tips The stems of caraway thyme root quickly where they touch the ground; combined with the plant's tolerance for heat and humidity, this layering trait helps ensure a long life in the garden. Plant caraway thyme in full sun. Like all thymes, it requires well drained soil to prevent rot. Work in sand, gravel, and compost as needed, but avoid adding sand to clay soils. Hardy in Zones 5 to 8.

Cultivars and Related Species Narrow-leafed *Thymus* 'TM95' (also called orange spice thyme) has a strong orange scent; *T. pulegioides* 'Tabor' has broader foliage; and *T. pulegioides* 'Doone Valley' is a creeping hybrid with yellow-splashed green leaves.

Companion Plants Weave an herbal carpet of lavender thyme (*Thymus thracicus*), the hot-pink-flowered elfin thyme (*T. doerfleri* 'Bressingham Pink'), silver thyme (*T.* 'Argenteus'), and gauzy-netted cobweb houseleek (*Sempervivum arachnoideum*).

A Garden of Culinary Herbs

Gwen Barclay and Madalene Hill

Culinary herbs can find a place anywhere in the garden: alongside fragrant antique roses, surrounding flowering shrubs and small trees, or interplanted with vegetables. Place the hardy rosemary 'Arp' (*Rosmarinus officinalis* 'Arp') at the front steps or either side of a gate to welcome guests with its heady fragrance. Green and golden lemon thymes (*Thymus* × *citriodorus*) make a charming border, especially spilling over stone or wooden edging. The much maligned curly parsley (*Petroselinum crispum* var. *crispum*) makes for a more upright border, and Italian, or flat-leafed, parsley (*Petroselinum crispum* var. *neapolitanum*) can create an airy enclosure around a small garden bed.

Use larger herbs to add interest to the landscape: Prune bay laurel (*Laurus nobilis*) into a pleasing single trunk, or let it grow into its natural shape with multiple main stems; encourage a young rosemary to greater stature by removing the lower branches; allow garden sage (*Salvia officinalis*) to soar above low-growing herbs. You can also place large containers of herbs directly in garden beds to raise the level of the landscape.

Use the design for an informal garden of culinary herbs on page 26 as an inspiration. You can adapt the garden's shape and size to suit the needs of a specific site, but it will be most effective if situated against a fence or wall. Use a hose to lay out the curve in a flowing manner that is pleasing to you and makes the most of the site. Make sure the tall bay laurel, or another large specimen plant such as an upright rosemary, is positioned off center in the long curving bed.

Continued on page 28

Attractive paving stones set off the herbs in the authors' large culinary herb garden. Raised beds bring up the level of the garden, giving the short plants some lift and keeping the delicate herb foliage dry and free from dirt.

A Culinary Herb Garden

The informal curving border of culinary herbs illustrated in the plan above is a relaxed and low-maintenance garden design. Well-draining soil and lots of sun are the only requirements. Be sure to locate the garden as close as possible to your kitchen so your favorite herbs will be close at hand and easy to pluck as you cook. And don't be stingy—plant each variety in generous groups of three or five or even more. Some good candidates for the culinary herb garden are profiled beginning on page 29. In this garden plan, a meandering path allows easy access to individual plants. A bay tree serves as a vertical accent, located off-center for interest. However, a fountain, sundial, or sculpture would work just as well. Keep in mind that even informal gardens require some structure. Repetition of key plants throughout the border can supply design logic in a subtle fashion. A border of parsley or other compact herb can help tie the garden together.

Growing Tips

- Most annual culinary herbs are easy to start from seed. Purchase perennial herbs as young plants from a reliable nursery for spring planting (or fall planting in hot climates).
- Pinch back herb seedlings and young nursery plants to encourage bushy growth.
- Harvest herbs regularly while they're in active growth to keep the plants in shape.
- Grow overexuberant mints in large containers to keep them from rampaging throughout the garden.
- Use balanced organic fertilizers, and use them sparely. Herbs don't need to be fed much, except when grown in pots in hot climates.
- Avoid pesticides—especially in a garden of herbs you intend to eat.

Plants Featured in This Garden

1 *Anethum graveolens*, dill
2 *Calendula officinalis*, pot marigold
3 *Coriandrum sativum*, coriander
4 *Elsholtzia ciliata*, Vietnamese balm
5 *Foeniculum vulgare* 'Rubrum', bronze fennel
6 *Laurus nobilis*, bay laurel
7 *Mentha × gracilis* 'Madalene Hill', doublemint
8 *Ocimum basilicum*, sweet basil
9 *Origanum majorana*, sweet marjoram
10 *Origanum × majoricum*, Italian oregano
11 *Petroselinum crispum*, Cilician parsley
12 *Petroselinum crispum* var. *crispum*, curly parsley
13 *Petroselinum crispum* var. *neapolitanum*, flat-leafed parsley

14 *Rosmarinus officinalis*, rosemary
15 *Salvia* 'Newe Ya'ar', 'Newe Ya'ar' garden sage
16 *Salvia officinalis* 'Purpurascens', purple sage
17 *Satureja biflora*, lemon savory
18 *Satureja montana*, winter savory
19 *Tagetes lucida*, Mexican tarragon
20 *Thymus × citriodorus*, lemon thyme
21 *Viola odorata*, sweet violet

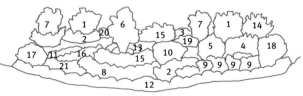

Follow your whims when designing an informal herb garden, but bear in mind that plants have different growing requirements. For best results, group moisture lovers, like the basil varieties above, together; pair drought-tolerant herbs such as thymes with other herbs that have the same needs.

There are no hard and fast rules for how to group plants, but it's a good idea to separate the herbs that like to be on the dry side, such as rosemary and thyme, from those that need to be watered often, like basil and parsley. Place herbs that you use regularly where they're easily accessible for quick harvest while you're cooking. It's also possible to grow all the herbs needed for an average family in two or three large whiskey barrels. (For more on growing herbs in pots, see "A Potted Herb Garden," page 62.) Using the culinary herbs regularly—every day in everything you prepare— keeps the plants well shaped and encourages tasty, tender foliage for cooking. Don't pay too much attention to the lovely hand-colored herb charts sold in shops that describe what herb to use with various foods. It is our theory that practically all culinary herbs work in practically any food, provided a light touch is used. Experiment with new flavors, perhaps adding a seasoning to a favorite recipe already in your repertoire that doesn't contain any herbs. Start with a small amount, noting how much you are using, and make adjustments next time. Better to have too little than too much. One advantage of fresh herbs is that it is almost impossible to overdo it; your eye will tell you when there is enough—the herbs should be flecked evenly throughout the food.

Herbs for a Kitchen Garden

Anethum graveolens
Dill

This beloved annual is a must in all herb gardens, and nothing beats the older varieties for flavor: 'Long Island Mammoth' and 'Vierling' produce large flower heads and grow to four feet. Strongly flavored 'Dukat' is nearly as tall. Both seeds and fronds, often called dill-weed, are used to make pickles, and the flower heads add flavor as well as beauty to the pickle jar. Chopped fronds are especially tasty in potato salads and with buttered new potatoes, cabbage, sauer-kraut, cucumbers, and salad dressings. Dill is also excellent with poultry, meat, and fish, as well as in soups and stews. Snip the tender flowers into salads.

Growing Tips In cold climates sow dill in early spring and repeat every few weeks or so to ensure a steady crop. In the South, dill is a cool-weather herb; plant it in fall and it will bloom in late spring, making

successive plantings difficult. Mature seeds will drop, and new plants will emerge the next season. Dill is a true annual.

Cultivars and Related Species The compact varieties *Anethum graveolens* 'Fernleaf' and 'Bouquet' are good for container growing. 'Hercules' and 'Tetra Leaf' are known for their good leaf production and are slow to bloom and seed.

Companion Plants Plant compact dill varieties such as 'Bouquet' and 'Fernleaf' as airy borders. Chervil (*Anthriscus cerefolium*), another cool-weather herb, likes the shade dill provides. Use tall varieties of dill and curly parsley (*Petroselinum crispum* var. *crispum*) together for an excellent border.

Coriandrum sativum
Coriander, Cilantro

The coriander plant usually grows one to three feet tall and produces bloom stalks with delicate white flowers before setting seeds. Coriander leaves, which are often called by their Spanish name, cilantro, are used in cuisines from Asia and Africa to Mexico, Central and South America, and the Caribbean. Since the essential oils dissipate quickly with heat, the leaves are generally used with fresh, uncooked foods such as relishes, salsas, and gua-camole or added to hot dishes just before serving. Green or unripe coriander seeds have much the same flavor as the leaves, but after maturing and drying, they develop a complex nutty, citrusy flavor and aroma and are delicious in many dishes, including desserts.

Growing Tips Grow coriander in full sun. In cold climates, sow coriander seed in early spring and repeat every few weeks throughout the season to ensure contin-

Anethum graveolens, dill.

uous harvest; in the South, plant in fall or late winter. Repeat plantings are usually not practical, as warm weather arrives too early. With warm temperatures, a jointed bloom stalk emerges, triggering ferny foliage, and seeds soon follow, usually within three weeks of sowing. Regular pruning of the bloom stalk may delay bolting for a short time. Coriander will generally reseed from year to year. It is a true annual.

Cultivars and Related Species *Coriandrum sativum* 'Leaf', 'Longstanding', 'Pot' (a new compact variety), and 'Santos' are highly touted as being slower to bolt. These claims may be valid in some areas, but in the South, where warm daytime temperatures can come as early as February and March, coriander does not get the message and quickly blooms.

Companion Plants Border coriander with deep green curly parsley (*Petroselinum crispum* var. *crispum*) or Italian oregano (*Origanum × majoricum*) for a nice show.

Elsholtzia ciliata
Vietnamese Balm, Rau Kinh Gioi

This perennial, used in Asian cuisines to impart a fresh lemon flavor, is a stunning addition to the kitchen garden. Vietnamese balm reaches up to 18 inches in height, with oval, roughly textured leaves and lovely dusky-pink flowers that grow in a three-inch-long whorl. The species name *ciliata* describes the many hairs (cilia) that give the leaves their distinctive roughness. Vietnamese balm's delightful fragrance enhances tomato and cucumber slices and uncooked sauces. Garnish soups and vegetables with it just before serving to impart a fine citrus aroma and flavor.

Growing Tips Grow Vietnamese balm in semishade or full sun in raised beds. Hardiness has not been established.

Cultivars and Related Species *Elsholtzia stauntonii* is a small subshrub growing to about two feet; its leaves have a strong mint fragrance. Hardy to Zone 4.

Companion Plants Vietnamese balm looks great in a container with curly parsley varieties such as *Petroselinum crispum* var. *crispum* 'Italian Dark Green' or 'Green River'.

Laurus nobilis
Bay Laurel, Sweet Bay, Grecian Bay

Sweet bay is the aristocrat of the herb garden, whether you plant it in a garden bed or grow it as a lovely container plant. It has a dense and shrubby growth habit and smooth, tough, glossy, bright green leaves. Fresh bay leaves and tender stems give an unbelievable richness to long-cooking soups or meaty stews. Bay in butter or olive oil is excellent with vegetables. You can also use

Coriandrum sativum, coriander.

Laurus nobilis, **bay laurel.**

bay in custards and puddings. When harvesting individual bay leaves, pull them down to expose the new leaf node; this will usually trigger growth of a new leaf or stem.

Growing Tips and Cultivars and Related Species See golden bay (*Laurus nobilis* 'Aurea'), page 17.

Mentha × *gracilis* 'Madalene Hill' Doublemint, Red-Stemmed Apple Mint, Red Mint

With stems that turn red when stressed by heat, cold, or limited supply of water, doublemint has a minty, fruity aroma and flavor and is our mint of choice for the kitchen. The rare combination of peppermint and spearmint flavors provides a balance of sweetness and pungency not present in other mints, making it especially suitable for savory recipes. Doublemint goes well in salad dressings, meat, grain, and vegetable dishes, and desserts of all types.

Growing Tips Grow culinary mints in large containers—the leaves will remain clean and the plants' aggressive tendencies can be controlled. You can also bury the pots in a bed with a healthy bit of rim sticking up. In the early spring and in mid-August remove all dead foliage and root-prune, cutting through both roots and stolons (prostrate or trailing stems) to stimulate new growth, or divide the plant. For the best flavor and more abundant foliage, do not permit mints to blossom. The hardiness range of doublemint has not been established. It is winter hardy in Zone 7, and with heavy mulch it likely is hardy in colder areas.

Cultivars and Related Species Of the many species, cultivars, and varieties of mint, the most important for culinary use are those with a strong, clear taste of spearmint (*Mentha* × *gracilis* and *M. spicata*). Many different clones of spearmint exist, a few of which have odious scents. Let your nose be your guide.

Orange mint (*Mentha aquatica*, page 44) is excellent for desserts, especially those made with citrus juice or zest.

Companion Plants All mints compete with other plants for space and water, and unless you carefully prune blossoms, some mints will cross-pollinate, resulting in seedlings with strange, muddy flavors. For these reasons, keep mints separated in their own containers and remove flower stalks. For a stunning look, try growing mints in tall chimney flues with a collection of lower containers surrounding them. Plant these with silvery variegated thyme (*Thymus × citriodorus* 'Silver Queen'), lavender-blue-flowering tricolor sage (*Salvia officinalis* 'Tricolor'), and perky calendulas.

Ocimum basilicum
Sweet Basil

Basil's pungent fragrance, strong flavor, and intense color make it almost everyone's favorite culinary herb. Basils often mimic the scent and taste of other

plants—cloves, cinnamon, anise, lemon, pepper, camphor, and menthol. Their leaves range from small and light green with smooth margins to large, purple, and ruffly, with all kinds of variations in between. Sweet basil (*Ocimum basilicum*) is a catchall term for the many sweet-scented varieties. The favored basils of Southeast Asia, for example, are slightly sweet and spicy but with less anise flavor than other varieties. They're delicate enough to enjoy in a broth-based soup yet will not be overpowered by the hot kick of chiles in curry dishes. 'Thai', 'True Thai', 'Thai Magic', and 'Sweet Thai' have purple flower spikes and stems that show off their crisp, shiny, dark green leaves. All basils volatilize, or release their essential oils, at very low temperatures, so add basil to hot food in the last stages of cooking or just as the dish is served.

Growing Tips See *Ocimum* cultivars, page 18.

Cultivars and Related Species *Ocimum basilicum* 'Lettuce Leaf', an excellent addition to salads, grows to about two feet with large leaves fragrant of licorice and cinnamon. *Ocimum × citriodorum* 'Aussie Sweetie' (also called 'Greek Column' and 'Lesbos') has fine flavor, dark green leaves, and an upright growth. *Ocimum americanum* 'Genoa Profumatissima' is considered one of the best basils for pesto; pepper basil (*O. selloi*), a three-foot species from Mexico, has the smell of fresh bell peppers. *Ocimum basilicum* 'Piccolo' has tiny leaves with a hint of mint and grows about two feet high; compact *O. basilicum* var. *thrysiflorum* 'Siam Queen', has deep purple, cone-shaped flower clusters.

A cultivar of *Ocimum basilicum*, sweet basil.

Origanum × majoricum, Italian oregano.

Companion Plants To complement basils' many shades of green and purple, plant them with bay laurel (*Laurus nobilis*, pages 17, 30) or green fennel (*Foeniculum vulgare*), or border them with creeping rosemary (*Rosmarinus officinalis* 'Blue Boy' or 'Dancing Waters'). Don't mix basils with herbs that need dry conditions such as lavenders or thymes.

Origanum × majoricum
Italian Oregano, Hardy Marjoram

Italian oregano is the oregano of choice in our kitchen. It is light and delicate yet speaks with authority. Italian oregano grows 15 to 18 inches tall. Prune it into balls or squares to make a statement in the garden or in a container, or grow it as a lovely, low-clipped hedge. When selecting an oregano plant for the kitchen, lightly brush its leaves with your fingers, then smell the plant, not your fingers. This will give you an idea of what the oregano will be like in your cooking.

Growing Tips Italian oregano is always grown from cuttings. It prefers well-draining soil and does well in full sun or partial shade. Though the tips may burn, it survives hard freezes, snow, and ice. Hardy to Zone 7.

Cultivars and Related Species Greek oregano (*Origanum vulgare* subsp. *hirtum*, page 56) is pungent to the nose and hot to the tongue; use it with a light touch. Many lovely oreganos have no fragrance whatsoever; they make excellent groundcovers but will do nothing for the marinara sauce, so for culinary purposes, stick with Italian oregano.

Companion Plants When allowed to reach its full height, Italian oregano combines well with a border of onion chives (*Allium schoenoprasum*) or English or French thyme (*Thymus vulgaris* 'Broadleaf English', page 60, 'Narrowleaf French', page 112). This oregano also makes a great border plant for taller upright rosemarys, flowering sages such as *Salvia leucantha*, and basils (*Ocimum basilicum* species and cultivars, pages 18, 32, 46, 68).

Petroselinum crispum
Cilician Parsley

At first glance you might think this new introduction to the herb lineup is plain old parsley, as its botanical name, which covers all parsleys, suggests. This plant is clearly different, and it will receive its own scientific name at some point. The young leaves are quite ferny or curly at first, but as the plant matures they come to resemble those of small, flat-leaved parsley or chervil (*Anthriscus cerefolium*)—yet Cilician parsley grows no taller than curly-leafed varieties. The leaves' aroma is sweet and their aftertaste almost citrusy. When grown in full sun the flavor seems to mimic the stronger taste of curly parsley. Best of all, the flavor does not tend to turn rank and bitter at the end of the season like other parsleys. Plants grow to about 12 inches

tall (36 inches with the bloom stalk), and if planted closely, they make a soft, airy groundcover. Cilician parsley is not widely available (try Heirloom Gardens, www.heirloomnursery.com).

Growing Tips Although Cilician parsley seems to grow well in full sun, its delicate, unique flavor suffers, so plant it where it gets some shade. The foliage is more delicate and fernlike when it is grown in partial shade; the flavor remains the same. Hardy in Zone 8; hardiness is not yet known for colder climes.

Cultivars and Related Species This parsley is related to curly-leafed types. Look for low-growing curly parsleys for border planting: *Petroselinum crispum* 'Starke' is a triple-curled selection, and 'Afrodite' is finely curled. 'Forest Green' and 'Extra Curled Dwarf' are more standard types.

Companion Plants Try this unusual plant in a container by itself, or use it with spring-flowering cheddar pinks (*Dianthus gratianopolitanus,* page 107), sweet violets (*Viola odorata*, page 98), and nasturtiums (*Tropaeolum*) in a lovely vignette.

Petroselinum crispum var. *neapolitanum*
Flat-Leafed, Italian, or Plain Parsley

The choice of cooks who strive for subtlety, flat-leaf parsley acts as a culinary liaison, allowing individual flavors to come through while melding them into a unified whole. Substitute Italian parsley for basil to make a fine pesto or herbal concentrate. Parsley is high in vitamins A, B, and C and a rich source of iron. Its high chlorophyll content provides the emerald-green color and acts as a breath freshener and palate cleanser. When a recipe calls for garlic, add parsley so the

Petroselinum crispum, Cilician parsley.

Petroselinum crispum var. *neapolitanum*, flat-leafed parsley, on the left. *Petroselinum crispum* var. *crispum*, curly parsley, on the right.

garlic won't talk back. Use the beautiful yellow blossoms in fresh bouquets.

Growing Tips Parsley likes full sun but will tolerate some high shade. You can grow Italian parsley from seed or purchase plants. It will grow to about 24 inches; the bloom stalks add a good 12 inches. Parsley is a biennial but usually treated as an annual. In the South it often flowers in the first year, particularly when grown from purchased plants, which were likely seeded in the fall, grown in heated greenhouses and pushed with fertilizers to saleable size. Hardy in Zones 6 to 9.

Cultivars and Related Species A new variety of flat-leaf parsley, *Petroselinum* var. *neapolitanum* 'Giant of Italy', is worth seeking out.

Companion Plants Plain parsley is tall enough to serve as a focal point in large containers with other herbs and flowers or combinedwith basil (*Ocimum basilicum* cultivars, pages 18, 32, 46, 68), zinnias, and other tall, flowering annuals during hot weather in cooler climates. Use it to screen the back of a garden bed behind smaller herbs such as thyme (*Thymus* species and cultivars, pages 23, 60, 71, 112), marjoram (*Origanum majorana*, page 56), and low-growing herbal flowers.

Rosmarinus officinalis
Rosemary

Rosemary, a perennial favorite among herb gardeners, announces its presence with a strong piney fragrance and flavor. Use it with care in the kitchen: It's very easy to use too much. Prostrate varieties grow 6 to 12 inches tall and serve as groundcovers and edgings. Upright types can reach several feet tall; they work well at the back of a border or as a potted centerpiece in the herb garden.

Rosmarinus officinalis, rosemary.

varieties 'Arp', 'Blue Spire', 'Dutch Mill', 'Madalene Hill', and 'Salem' are considered hardy to Zone 7, and may survive in colder areas with good winter protection. For tips on overwintering rosemary indoors, see *Rosmarinus officinalis* 'Joyce DeBaggio', page 47.

Cultivars and Related Species After testing, tasting, and inhaling both the flavor and aroma of many varieties of rosemary, we've narrowed our favorites for the kitchen to *Rosmarinus officinalis* 'Arp', 'Hill Hardy', 'Tuscan Blue', 'Gorizia', and 'Salem'. Interestingly, these varieties have lower levels of pinene and camphor.

Companion Plants Prostrate rosemarys such as *Rosmarinus officinalis* 'Blue Boy' or 'Huntington Carpet' make a spectacular sight spilling over stone or brick walls and down terraced hillsides. Upright rosemary makes a strong statement in the garden or in a large container. 'Benenden Blue', 'Blue Spire', or 'Gorizia' are lovely surrounded by lower-growing purple sage (*Salvia officinalis* 'Purpurascens') or golden sage (Salvia officinalis 'Icterina'), small-leafed basils such as *Ocimum* × *citriodorum* 'Spicy Globe' or creeping golden oregano (*Origanum vulgare* 'Aureum', page 19).

Growing Tips Rosemary requires excellent drainage. It is quite drought-tolerant once established but needs supplementary water if rain is sparse. Start rosemary from cuttings, as seed germination is slow and varieties will not come true from seed. To prevent the troublesome disease *Pseudonymous syringae* (rosemary stemgall or stemknot) in areas where it is prevalent, use Mediterranean mulch (see box on page 61) and prune away affected parts (stems with growths resembling root knobs). Even hardy varieties (see below) need protection from icy winds in winter: Wrap them in floating row covers or cloth, never plastic; use cedar and pine boughs to create walls and lean-tos that support rosemary under snow and ice. At the base of south-facing walls, rosemary enjoys shelter and stored solar heat. Prune away freeze-damaged branches in spring. Once established, the

Salvia 'Newe Ya'ar' (*S. officinalis* × *S. fruticosa*) 'Newe Ya'ar' Garden Sage

Trying to grow common sage, *Salvia officinalis*, through the summer months in the humid South is like trying to toss that proverbial snowball in Hades. The gray furry leaves of sage indicate the plant's adaptation to full sun and good drainage and signal its intolerance for humid heat. However, 'Newe Ya'ar' (pronounced noy yar), a cultivar from Israel, not only tolerates humidity but seems to thrive on it. And it has a lighter, more pleasant aroma and taste than other sages: According to research, 'Newe Ya'ar' has much less camphor than common sage (*Salvia officinalis*).

Growing Tips This is a big plant, so give it room to grow. 'Newe Ya'ar' sage blooms profusely in the spring with the typical lavender-blue flowers of the species. Grown in full sun, it develops into a stunning two- to three-foot-tall plant; in high shade, it sprawls a bit but still grows well. Relatively new to North America, this sage's hardiness has not been established. It can safely overwinter in Zone 8, and maybe Zone 7 with protection.

Cultivars and Related Species *Salvia officinalis* 'Icterina', 'Tricolor', or 'Purpurascens' have a "sausage sage" flavor. Autumn sage (*S. greggii*) and red-flowering pineapple sage (*S. elegans*, page 47) are also flavorful and traditionally used in food (pineapple sage shouldn't be heated).

Companion Plants Grow *Salvia* 'Newe Ya'ar' with golden-leafed herbs such as *Origanum vulgare* 'Aureum' or any of the golden-leafed thymes, such as *Thymus* × *citriodorus* 'Aureus', page 49, or flowering herbs for a silver and gold theme.

Satureja biflora
Lemon savory

This small-leafed savory is a little-known culinary jewel with a fine citrus fragrance. Growing only about 15 inches high in full sun, it can easily be covered by more vigorously growing neighbors, so plant accordingly. Toss the lemony leaves in a green salad or use them in a salad dressing or vinaigrette. All citrus fragrances volatilize quickly with heat, so use lemon savory in cold or uncooked dishes and add it to hot vegetables and sauces just before serving.

Growing Tips Lemon savory grows well in containers. Hardiness has not been established in North America for this relatively new addition but it is hardy in the warmer parts of Zone 8.

Cultivars and Related Species Winter savory (*Satureja montana*, page 59) is a fine, dependable kitchen herb with tiny, stiff, dark green foliage. Its hot peppery flavor speaks with authority, so only a few leaves are needed. Summer savory (*S. hortensis*, page 22), a popular culinary herb, is a tender annual and not happy in climates with long, hot summers.

Companion Plants Plant lemon savory with low-growing thymes (*Thymus* species and cultivars, pages 23, 60, 71, 112) and oreganos; it also does well in a container on its own.

Salvia 'Newe Ya'ar', 'Newe Ya'ar' garden sage.

An Herb Garden for Tea Time

Susan Belsinger and Tina Marie Wilcox

People around the world have been creating tea gardens for as long as they have been drinking tea. In China and Japan, the tradition dates back not just centuries but millennia. Eastern cultures have long appreciated the psychological and spiritual importance of creating contemplative places for sipping tea. In Europe tea gardens are also a venerable tradition. For hundreds of years the English, famous tea drinkers, have cultivated herbs in formal and cottage gardens and appreciated their harvest in that most celebrated of cultural rituals, afternoon tea.

In our frenetically paced modern lives, making time for growing herbs and savoring herbal infusions may seem like an anachronism, a quaint throwback to a more unhurried age. But we need such time-tested tonics, places to slow down and enjoy nature's bounty, seemingly more than ever. The garden on page 40 is tailored to modern gardeners and tea lovers who lead busy lives. Below is advice on how to enjoy the pleasures of harvesting and drying fragrant and flavorful herbs for tea.

Harvesting and Drying Herbs

Most herbs should be harvested just before they bloom. Choose a sunny day and harvest in the morning, when the herbs' oils are strongest. Never pick herbs when they are wet; wait until the morning dew has evaporated. Don't leave cut herbs out in the sun; take them into a shady area to sort and tie into bunches.

Continued on page 42

Over time, your tastebuds will inform the character of your tea garden as you add more of your favorite herbs and grow less of others.

An Herb Garden for Tea Time

A tea garden can be designed in any number of shapes and configurations, from informal and cottage garden–style to formal and symmetrical to zenlike. You can also get as imaginative and whimsical as you wish, as in the garden plan here. This tea garden has been designed in the shape of a homey teapot; however, one or two teacups, complete with saucers, could also be fun. The teapot measures 8 to 10 feet from lid to bottom, and 10 to 12 feet from handle to spout. This is roomy enough to accommodate 15 to 20 plants, generously spaced. In your own yard, adequate space and sunlight will be the only limitations; just remember that the larger the herb garden, the more maintenance it will require. Time, space, and your tastebuds will dictate how many plants of a given variety you need to grow to have plenty of leaves and flowers on hand to brew your favorite cup; some recommendations begin on page 43.

Design Tips

• Tea gardens should be places for relaxation and reflection. The sense of calm can be accentuated by creating a feeling of enclosure in the garden. This can be accomplished with traditional hedges, trellises or wooden fences, or even rows of good-sized plant specimens in pots.

• Make room in your garden for a tea table and chairs or benches where you can sip your freshly brewed herbal tonic.

• Tea paraphernalia used as garden ornament can add an entertaining touch. For example, try edging a bed with some old teaspoons or mismatched saucers turned on end. Or attach old teacups to garden stakes and use them as plant markers.

• As in any garden in which plants are intended to be eaten, be sure to grow your tea garden organically.

Plants Featured in This Garden

1 *Aloysia citriodora*, lemon verbena

2 *Matricaria recutita*, German chamomile

3 *Melissa officinalis*, lemon balm

4 *Mentha aquatica*, orange mint

5 *Mentha spicata*, spearmint

6 *Monarda didyma* 'Cambridge Scarlet', red-flowered bee balm

7 *Ocimum* 'Mrs. Burns' Lemon', 'Mrs. Burns' Lemon' basil

8 *Rosmarinus* species, rosemarys

9 *Salvia elegans*, pineapple sage

10 *Salvia* species, sages

11 *Stevia rebaudiana*, stevia

12 *Thymus* × *citriodorus* 'Aureus', golden lemon thyme

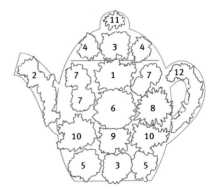

In cold-winter areas the last harvest should be six to eight weeks before the first hard freeze to give perennials time to harden off new growth. At your final harvest, cut annuals to the ground and cut back perennials to about two thirds of their height.

To dry herbs, tie the stalks into small bundles with string or twine and hang them up. You can also spread the herbs on screens or in baskets. Leave small or needlelike leaves like those of thyme and rosemary on their stems, but remove large leaves from stalks. Place the bundles, screens, or baskets in a dry, well-ventilated place out of the sun, such as a shed or attic. Depending on the climate and humidity, drying can take from a few days to two weeks. Check the herbs every day; if you leave them too long, especially in humid weather, they will turn brown.

Alternatively, you can use your refrigerator to dry herbs. Simply place small bundles of freshly harvested herbs in paper bags, label them, and place the partially closed bags on a shelf. The fridge-drying process is slow—about two weeks, depending upon the thickness of the leaves—but worth the wait. In the cool environment and relative darkness of the refrigerator, herb leaves retain valuable essential oils and more chlorophyll. You can completely dry the herbs in the fridge and then use them from the bag as needed. Or, remove all excess moisture and store them in a cool, dark place.

A fully dried herb will crackle and crumble when rubbed between your fingers. If the leaves are not crisp, they still contain some moisture. To remove the last bit of excess moisture and completely dry the herbs, finish them in the oven. Preheat the oven to its lowest temperature, but definitely under 200°F, and then turn it off. Spread the herbs on baking sheets and place them in the warm oven for about five minutes. Repeat if necessary.

Once the herbs are completely dried, strip whole leaves from the stems and pack

them in clean, dark-glass jars with tight-fitting lids. (Incompletely dried herbs will get moldy and spoil.) Don't crumble the leaves as you pack them or you'll release their essential oils.

At planting time, envision the shape perennial herbs take once they are established. Give ground-hugging Roman chamomile—leaves, flowers, and tea at left—a place to roam.

Herbs for a Tea Garden

Aloysia citriodora
Lemon Verbena

Lemon verbena has the most assertive fragrance and flavor of all the lemony herbs. Its strong, sweet citrus aroma and lemon-rind flavor make it a wonderful choice for tea. The plant has woody stems with narrow, pointed, bright green leaves. In southern regions or in a green-house it may grace you with white flowers tinged with lavender.

Growing Tips Lemon verbena requires full sun and a porous, loamy soil. Grow it in a protected spot even in warm climates and cultivate it in a pot north of Zone 8. Propagate from new-growth cuttings taken in late spring, or start from root cuttings in moistened sterilized soilless mix. Fertilize it with fish emulsion, prune judiciously during the growing season, and prune well in early fall. Remove about a third of the total plant, pruning smaller branches back to older growth. Lemon verbena drops its leaves when cold weather arrives. Mulch it for winter protection if its stays outdoors or move it into a cool greenhouse. Water it lightly in winter. Hardy in Zones 8 to 10.

Cultivars and Related Species None.

Companion Plants Group lemon verbena with basil (*Ocimum basilicum* cultivars, pages 18, 32, 46), the spiky flowers of pineapple sage (*Salvia elegans*), and the furry foliage of fruit-scented and ornamental sages (*Salvia* species and cultivars, pages 36, 47, 58, 111). The woody stems and pale green leaves combine well with the variegated foliage of Alaska nasturtiums (*Tropaeolum majus* cultivars).

Aloysia citriodora, lemon verbena.

Matricaria recutita
German Chamomile

Chamaemelum nobile
Roman Chamomile

The plants of both genera have ferny green foliage with small daisylike flowers. In tea, the flowers have a mild, sweet, fruity taste, but those of Roman chamomile (syn. *Anthemis nobilis*) have slightly more bitter components. Walking on a mat of Roman chamomile, a perennial groundcover, is an aromatic experience. Drinkng tea made from the plant may cause allergic reactions in those sensitive to ragweed (*Ambrosia artemisiifolia*).

Growing Tips Ground-hugging Roman chamomile spreads slowly over time, sending up bloom stalks that can reach 10 or 12 inches. Propagate it by seed, layering, or cuttings. Sow German chamomile in spring or fall. The upright plants grow about 10 to 12 inches tall and can flower two to three times a year. Both species like well-drained, loamy, moist soil and full sun; Roman chamomile can tolerate some shade. Gather the blooms when they first open and use them fresh, or preserve them by freezing or drying. Hardy in Zones 4 to 9.

Cultivars and Related Species *Chamaemelum nobile* 'Treneague' is a fragrant groundcover that does not bloom; *C. nobile* 'Flore Pleno' has showy white ruffly double blooms.

Companion Plants Set chamomile between stones or bricks along the edge of a walkway with other low growers, or allow its foliage to tangle with that of love-in-a-mist (*Nigella*) or brightly colored nasturtiums (*Tropaeolum*).

Melissa officinalis
Lemon Balm

The fragrances of lemon and honey mingle in lemon balm's leaves. Patches of the 2- to 2½-foot-tall plant attract large numbers of bees, especially when it's in bloom. Lemon balm contributes a subtly sweet, grassy flavor and a hint of lemon to a variety of dishes. Steep the crushed fresh leaves with iced tea or lemonade to make a delicious hot-weather beverage; in winter, the dried leaves make a nice hot tea, though some of the herb's aroma is lost in drying.

Growing Tips Lemon balm thrives in full sun but will grow in partial shade. Start it from seed, root cuttings, or by root division. It prefers light soil but will grow in heavy clay if it is amended with compost. Give each plant two feet all around. Trim during the growing season to keep it bushy. Hardy in Zones 4 to 9.

Cultivars and Related Species *Melissa officinalis* 'Aurea' and 'All Gold', two variegated cultivars, add color with their yellow-and-green leaves. Cut 'Aurea' back in the summer since its colors fade. 'All Gold' will burn in full summer sun.

Companion Plants Since lemon balm spreads easily and will compete for space, plant it next to other vigorous perennials such as mints (*Mentha* cultivars, pages 31, 44) or alliums, such as *Allium senescens* subsp. *montanum*, page 16, or *A. cernuum*, page 106).

Mentha aquatica
Orange Mint

Also called bergamot, water mint, and eau de cologne mint, orange mint is highly perfumed with a strong citrus flavor, but unlike other mints, it has very little menthol. This lovely plant has ovate leaves tinged purple on the underside and lavender-pink flowers. It grows to between two and three feet tall. The delightful flavor of orange mint is delicious in iced drinks and exceptional in fruit preserves and desserts. All mints are so good in tea blends that it's worth growing more than one type. Used in

Melissa officinalis, lemon balm.

Monarda didyma 'Cambridge Scarlet', red-flowered bee balm.

cold-water infusions they make wonderfully refreshing beverages.

Growing Tips Cut back plants and gather herbs for drying two to three times during the season; cut plants to the ground at the fall harvest. Hardy in Zones 5 to 9. For more tips, see *Mentha × gracilis* 'Madalene Hill', page 31.

Cultivars and Related Species Peppermints, the strongest-flavored mints, are high in menthol and make a stimulating tea. Look for *Mentha × piperita* 'Mitcham's' (syn. 'Blue Balsam', 'Chocolate', and 'Black-Stemmed Peppermint'). Doublemint (*M. × gracilis* 'Madalene Hill', page 31) combines the flavor of peppermint and spearmint and makes a great tea. Spearmints (*Mentha spicata*) have a milder, sweeter flavor than peppermints; 'Kentucky Colonel' is a favorite.

Companion Plants Due to their aggressive nature, it's best to confine mints to large pots or tubs.

Monarda didyma 'Cambridge Scarlet' Red-Flowered Bee Balm, Bergamot, Oswego Tea

Bees and hummingbirds are drawn to the strong aroma and nectar of red-flowered bee balm's brilliant, shaggy blooms. 'Cambridge Scarlet' grows from two to four feet tall and has a pleasantly strong sweet and flowery taste with citrus undertones. Both flowers and leaves make a delightful beverage and are great with summer fruits and desserts.

Growing Tips Sow seeds in spring or start plants by root division or cuttings. Plant bee balm in sun or partial shade, in loamy soil. Harvest the leaves and flowers throughout the season to use fresh or to dry. Some bee balms are susceptible to powdery mildew, which usually occurs later in the growing season, so harvest a few times early in the season to ensure a harvest to dry. Hardy in Zones 4 to 9.

Cultivars and Related Species Other varieties such as *Monarda didyma* 'Croftway Pink', 'Mahogany', 'Marshall's Delight', and wild bergamot (*M. fistulosa*, page 83) do not have the same fragrance or taste as the red varieties. They are gorgeous nectar plants, but they contain carvacrol, which gives them a pungent, savory taste similar to oregano.

Companion Plants Bee balms are in the mint family and tend to spread when grown in rich soils. The bright red flowers of *Monarda didyma* 'Cambridge Scarlet' are wonderful in a mass on their own or grouped with other tall plants such as oriental lilies and coneflowers (*Echinacea*).

Ocimum 'Mrs. Burns' Lemon'
'Mrs. Burns' Lemon' Basil

All of the lemon basils have a sweet lemon scent and a first taste of lemon oil with floral tones. Leaves and flowers are delicious in hot or iced tea and lemonade, as well as many other dishes. 'Mrs. Burns' Lemon', a cross between *Ocimum basilicum* and *O. americanum*, is a sturdy variety with good lemon fragrance and flavor; 'Sweet Dani' runs a close second. The plants have light, bright green leaves with small white blossoms.

Growing Tips See Greek bush basil (*Ocimum basilicum* 'Minimum', page 18). Harvest monthly by cutting plants back to just above the bottom two sets of leaves; this will vastly increase your yield.

Cultivars and Related Species Tasting of spice, citrus, and a hint of anise, favorite basils for tea include *Ocimum* × *citriodorum* 'Aussie Sweetie' (syn. 'Greek Column' and 'Lesbos') and Thai basils *O. basilicum* 'Siam Queen', 'True Thai', and 'Thai Purple'.

Companion Plants Combine tall columnar, bright green *O. basilicum* 'Aussie

Ocimum 'Mrs. Burns' Lemon', 'Mrs. Burns' Lemon' basil.

Sweetie' with the light green leaves of 'Mrs. Burns' Lemon' and the dark green foliage and bright purple flowers of 'True Thai' for a striking grouping.

Rosmarinus officinalis 'Joyce DeBaggio'
Golden Rain Rosemary

Unique among rosemary varieties, the leaves of the cultivar 'Joyce DeBaggio', named for the wife of herb grower Thomas DeBaggio, are edged in gold. This upright plant with pale blue flowers is tender in northern gardens, but in southern climates it grows like a shrub, reaching up to six feet in height and diameter. It has a resinous and piney aroma and flavor, with hints of citrus. Use the flowers to garnish beverages and desserts. Rosemary tea made from leaves and flowers of any cultivar is restorative, stimulating, and an aid to digestion.

Rosmarinus officinalis 'Joyce DeBaggio', golden rain rosemary.

Growing Tips To overwinter container-grown rosemary inside in cool climates, keep it as cool and dormant as possible. Restrict water to avoid fungal diseases, but don't allow the plant to dry out completely. For more growing tips, see *Rosmarinus officinalis*, page 35.

Cultivars and Related Species See pages 35, 57, 70.

Companion Plants Any rosemary companions such as thymes, oreganos, and savory should be spaced so that they don't touch the foliage.

Salvia elegans • Pineapple Sage

This elegant, sweetly scented tender perennial grows to a large bushy plant that can reach about four feet tall and three feet wide in the South. Pineapple sage's scarlet flower spikes appear very late in summer, and in southern climates, the plant blooms for up to three months. If you move the plant indoors in late fall in northern climates, it may bloom for a few months. When rubbed or brushed, the pointed leaves smell of fruity pineapple. Popular with hummingbirds, the brilliant, long-throated flowers have a sweet, strong floral aroma reminiscent of pineapple. Use them in preserves, desserts, and fruit salads and to brighten iced teas and other beverages.

Growing Tips Pineapple sage grows best in full sun in rich, slightly acidic soil. It is slow to germinate and therefore best propagated by cuttings or root divisions. Unless you live in a warm climate, grow it in a pot and move it to a sunny spot indoors when it gets cold. Hardy in Zones 8 to 11.

Cultivars and Related Species Tender *Salvia dorisiana*, also known as fruit-scented sage, has big fuzzy heart-shaped leaves and makes a lovely fruity tea.

Salvia elegans, pineapple sage.

honey and a slice of lemon. Or use it as a cold-water infusion.

Growing Tips Plant drought-tolerant hardy sages in well-drained or gravelly soil and full sun or in partial shade with good air circulation. Add calcium if it's lacking in the soil. Once established, sage needs little care; prune in early spring to encourage new growth, and water occasionally. Hardy in Zones 5 to 8.

Cultivars and Related Species *Salvia* 'Albiflora' has white flowers; 'Berggarten' has large round pungent leaves; 'Nana' has a wonderful growing habit and small leaves. Garden sage (*S. officinalis* × *S. fruticosa* 'Newe Ya'ar', page 36) tolerates humidity much better than other sages.

Companion Plants Given plenty of space, gray-green sage combines beautifully with any white-blooming flower. It looks good with other purple-blooming herbs such as chives (*Allium schoenoprasum*), lavender (*Lavandula,* pages 55, 109), and anise hyssop (*Agastache foeniculum*). The variegated pale green leaves of 'Woodcote Farm' sage look good with the white blooms of garlic chives (*Allium tuberosum)* or a white-flowering rose or bee balm (*Monarda*). Or try it with the fuzzy silver leaves of lamb's ears (*Stachys byzantina*).

Companion Plants The bright colors of marigolds (*Tagetes* species and cultivars, pages 70, 111), calendulas, nasturtiums (*Tropaeolum*), coleuses, and miniature chile plants (*Capsicum* species) are wonderful around pineapple sage.

Salvia officinalis 'Woodcote Farm'
'Woodcote Farm' Sage

A beautiful specimen with two-toned leaves and a faint gray-green variegation, 'Woodcote Farm' sage is welcome in the many-shades-of-green herb garden. Depending on soil and weather conditions, sage may vary in flavor, but camphor is prominent as well as a lemony resinous taste. When sage is dried, the lemon flavor dissipates and camphor and muskiness similar to silage comes forth. Despite its camphorous flavor, tea made from sage can be soothing and pleasant with a drop of

Stevia rebaudiana
Stevia

Also known as Paraguayan sweet herb and "yerba dulce," this shrubby tender perennial grows to about 18 inches tall, with tiny white flowers appearing at stem tips in summer. The two-inch, bright green leaves contain stevioside, which can be 100 to 300 times sweeter than sucrose. Paraguayans use it to sweeten bitter drinks like maté and, along with Japanese, Chinese, Korean, and Brazilian cooks, use it for pickles, desserts, and beverages.

Growing Tips Plant stevia in full sun and well-drained soil. This grass- and marshland native prefers some moisture and will not tolerate drought. Propagate by taking stem cuttings before flowers appear. When overwintering stevia, watch the leaves for pests, fertilize monthly, and prune away weak growth. Hardy in Zones 9 to 10.

Cultivars and Related Species There are many species in the genus, but *Stevia rebaudiana* has the sweetest leaf.

Companion Plants Grow stevia alone in a container or grouped with other sun-loving plants.

Thymus × *citriodorus* 'Aureus'
Golden Lemon Thyme

French and English thyme may be good for cooking, but lemon thymes are best for tea. They grow in compact little bushes 6 to 12 inches in height and come in a variety of leaf colors from green to gold to variegated. 'Aureus' (or 'Gold Edge'), has green leaves splashed with gold. Its foliage is showy in winter and spring in southern regions, and in early summer it puts forth pink flowers. Lemon thymes have a wonderful citrusy scent and flavor along with a whisper of rose and make a delightful tea. Add the leaves fresh to the teapot for maximum flavor. Dried leaves are less intense but still make a good tea and combine well with other tea herbs.

Growing Tips Mulch plants with sand, light-colored gravel, or chicken grit to keep them dry and discourage disease and mildew. Prune several times a year to prevent disease and keep plants from getting woody, first in early spring, again when flowers begin to form, then in midsummer, and finally about 60 days before first frost. Plants tend to die out

Stevia rebaudiana, stevia.

from the center. Pruning the tips stimulates new growth from the remaining lower sections, promoting vigorous, bushy specimens. Divide plants in spring or early fall and take root cuttings in summer. Hardy in Zones 5 to 9.

Cultivars and Related Species All cultivars of *Thymus* × *citriodorus* have a lovely lemony scent and flavor. 'Silver Queen' has paler, silver leaves, and 'Archer's Gold' has bright yellow leaves. 'Orange Balsam' has an orange fragrance and flavor.

Companion Plants Thymes are best with other low-growing plants that need good drainage. Use them with cheddar pinks (*Dianthus gratianopolitanus*, page 107), germander (*Teucrium chamaedrys*, page 23), lavenders, and savory (*Satureja* species, pages 22, 37, 59). Thyme also looks nice growing around rocks and along border edges.

A Gray-and-Green Garden of Mediterranean Herbs

Susan Belsinger and Tina Marie Wilcox

Taking its inspiration from the chalky, gritty, and barren landscapes that are a prevalent feature of arid natural areas in the Mediterranean basin, the garden of gray and green herbs shown on page 52 contrasts with lush cottage gardens. In its sparseness, it emulates the harsh growing conditions in the plants' native habitats, where water is precious, growth is slow, and the characteristic foliage comes in muted shades of gray and green, displayed on short, stocky plants, sculpted by wind and sun. To get into the spirit of things, try observing native plant communities and follow nature's cues when laying out your garden of Mediterranean herbs.

Setting the Stage for Mediterranean Herbs

Choose a site for your Mediterranean garden that receives a minimum of six hours of sunlight a day and is elevated. Avoid low-lying ground where puddles stand for more than an hour after a hard rain. Then do a percolation test to check how fast water seeps into the soil. Dig a hole and fill it with water: If the water doesn't drain away very quickly—say in ten minutes or so—improve the drainage; otherwise, consider creating a Mediterranean container garden. Mark off the outer border of the entire garden with string and then completely remove all plant life within; as you work the

Continued on page 54

Located close to the house, this Mediterranean-inspired herb garden is ready for close inspection, which is the perfect way for admiring a garden that showcases small plants.

A Garden of Mediterranean Herbs

The garden plan above is inspired by the harsh but beautiful natural habitat of the Mediterranean region, bleached by the sun and adapted to drought. Texture and negative space are the essence of this garden. Resinous, leathery needles, dense, clustered foliage, and soft, down-covered and pebbled leaves—all adaptations to conserve precious water—dominate the scenery. The plant colors are gentle on the eye: The muted palette ranges from dark green rosemary to gray-green sage, silvery oregano, gray santolina, and blue-gray lavender. These Mediterranean herbs are small, wonderfully aromatic shrubs that take on pleasing mound or windswept forms as they mature. As in their native habitat, the plants are widely spaced, given lots of room so they remain drenched in sun and air can circulate freely through their branches. After the long dry season, Mediterranean gardens appear gray and very rugged, but they soften up as the return of rain stimulates bursts of fresh foliage, heralding the arrival of the delicate flowers that will add a dash of color throughout the growing season.

Design Tips

- Create negative space in the Mediterranean garden by judiciously placing rocks, boulders, and gritty mulch among the plants.

- Cover the ground between the plants with a gritty, reflective mulch of sand and coarser light green, gray, burnt-orange, and white minerals. For details, see page 61.

- Make sure the soil in your garden of Mediterranean herbs drains thoroughly, or these drought-adapted plants will rot.

- One way to provide a well-drained substrate for Mediterranean herbs is to plant them in raised beds. You can arrange these beds in a terraced design, a nod to the ancient cultural landscapes of the region.

Plants Featured in This Garden

1 *Lavandula angustifolia*, lavender

2 *Origanum majorana*, sweet marjoram

3 *Origanum vulgare* subsp. *hirtum* 'Kalitera', 'Kalitera' oregano

4 *Rosmarinus officinalis* 'Majorca Pink', 'Majorca Pink' rosemary

5 *Salvia officinalis* 'Nana', 'Nana' sage

6 *Santolina chamaecyparissus*, gray santolina

7 *Santolina pinnata*, green santolina

8 *Satureja montana*, winter savory

9 *Thymus vulgaris* 'Broadleaf English', 'Broadleaf English' thyme

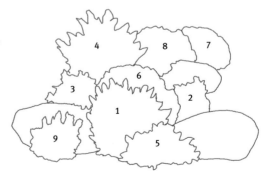

Subtle colors, forms, and textures unite to create a pleasing design, inspired by natural and man-made landscapes of the Mediterranean region.

soil, pick out any wireworms, grubs, and cutworms you find. A clean start will reduce weed competition and pest problems in future years. Next, mark off each individual bed with string. Transfer the top four inches of soil from the path onto the growing areas to create raised beds. You can refill the path with bark, stone, bricks, or shell. Raised beds drain well and keep fungal diseases at bay. While you're making raised beds, also consider installing soaker hoses, an efficient watering system that promotes plant health by keeping foliage dry.

Cover the beds with reflective inorganic mulch: A mixture of crushed oyster shells, minerals, and coarse sand works well. (For a recipe, see page 61.) Avoid bark, straw, or other plant-based mulches, which may contribute to the spread of deadly fungal diseases.

Caring for Mediterranean Herbs

When you first plant Mediterranean herbs, water them carefully to help them establish new roots. During the hot, dry summer months, water them deeply once a week, preferably in the early morning. Avoid wetting the leaves in the heat of the day, as the water droplets can magnify light rays and cause leaf burn. Also avoid watering in the evening—fungal diseases spread easily on foliage that stays wet overnight. Apply fish emulsion and liquid kelp during the growing season. Bear in mind, though, that Mediterranean plants are endemic to poor, chalky soils and will have higher concentrations of essential oils if they are not overfertilized, particularly with nitrogen. In winter, water only as needed to keep the soil from drying out completely. Soggy soil promotes the spread of disease, and water left standing around the roots may cause the plants to suffocate.

Herbs for a Mediterranean Garden

Lavandula angustifolia 'Royal Velvet'
'Royal Velvet' Lavender

This pretty, diminutive selection produces deep purple flower spikes that retain their color when dried. 'Royal Velvet' reaches only about 12 inches in height when in flower and fits well into small spaces.

Growing Tips Lavender needs excellent drainage and air circulation, especially in hot, humid climates, where it is prone to sudden wilts. Purchase plants from a reputable grower, or start with root cuttings taken in late spring and early summer. In the spring, when new growth appears, remove winter damage. After flowering, prune away spent flower stems and judiciously thin dense growth to improve air circulation. Hardy in Zones 5 to 8. In colder areas, overwinter lavender in a cool greenhouse.

Cultivars and Related Species Most lavender species and hybrids grow from one to three feet tall, with blossoms ranging from lavender to white and pink on flower spikes that can reach four feet in some varieties. *Lavandula angustifolia* is the best lavender for culinary use—but only its flowers are safe to eat. Do not consume the foliage or essential oil. *Lavandula angustifolia* 'Hidcote', a dwarf variety, has deep purple flowers. 'Munstead' is grown for its aster-purple flower spikes and semi-dwarf habit. 'Short and Sweet' syn. 'Susan Belsinger', a smaller selection, has six-inch flower spikes with a delicious aroma; it's rare but worth the search. *Lavandula dentata*, fringe-leaf lavender, is furry, pale green-gray with toothed leaves and flat, conical spikes. *Lavandula stoechas*, French

lavender, (sometimes called Spanish lavender) has an open, erect, spreading habit and can winter outside in warmer areas of Zones 7 to 9. Leaves are narrow and pale blue-gray; flower buds form a thick, dark purple cone capped with unusual bright purple bracts.

Companion Plants Lavender is picky about companions and doesn't like to be touched. To fill in blank spots while small lavenders are growing to maturity, choose diminutive, cool-season annuals. *Lobelia* 'Crystal Blue' has pretty flowers that echo lavender's blooms; it will die as temperatures rise in the summer, allowing all-important air circulation around the lavenders. Use creeping thymes such as caraway thyme (*Thymus herba-barona*, page 23) to carpet the ground around lavenders. They generally seek sun and should not threaten the health of lavender by encroachment.

Lavandula × intermedia 'Grosso'
'Grosso' Lavandin

Lavandins, the offspring of a cross between *Lavandula angustifolia* from the

Lavandula × *intermedia* 'Grosso', 'Grosso' lavandin.

mountains and *L. latifolia* from lower elevations, are bred for disease resistance and high essential-oil content. *Lavandula × intermedia* 'Grosso', an excellent selection for southern gardeners, has vigorous, rounded growth with dense foliage. The flower spikes are branched and have stems up to 14 inches long. Like most lavandins, 'Grosso' is large in width and girth. Though beautiful in the garden, the lavandins are higher in camphor and eucalyptol than *Lavandula angustifolia*, and their blossoms are not good to eat.

Growing Tips and Companion Plants See *Lavandula angustifolia*, 'Royal Velvet', page 55. Hardy in Zones 5 to 7.

Cultivars and Related Species *Lavandula × intermedia* 'Fred Boutin' has beautiful silver foliage, even in the winter landscape. Plants grow to almost three feet wide and are somewhat disease-resistant.

Origanum majorana
Sweet Marjoram

Sweet marjoram is a tender perennial that with regular trimming grows into a handsome, petite bush with thin stems, small greenish-gray leaves, and tiny white flowers in mid- to late summer. Harvest marjoram in summer and fall to use fresh; preserve it by cutting the herb stems and drying them on screens or by tying them in bunches and hanging in a warm, dry place. Dried marjoram retains its sweet aroma.

Growing Tips Sweet marjoram is best propagated by root cuttings. If you start from seed, be certain that you have *Origanum majorana*. In cooler regions, overwinter plants in a greenhouse or on a sunny windowsill in well-drained pots. Hardy in Zones 9 to 10.

Cultivars and Related Species Italian oregano, also known as hardy marjoram (*Origanum × majoricum*, page 33), is believed to be a cross between *O. majorana* and *O. vulgare* subsp. *virens*. It is a favorite in gardens and kitchens.

Companion Plants The white variegation of 'Silver Queen' lemon thyme (*Thymus × citriodorus* 'Silver Queen') sets off the green-gray foliage and white flower buds of sweet marjoram. Use heartsease (*Viola tricolor*) in early spring to fill the future growing space. Its edible flowers are charming and colorful.

Origanum vulgare subsp. *hirtum*
'Kalitera'
'Kalitera' Oregano

If you like oregano that is hardy, slow to flower, and keeps its place in the garden, choose 'Kalitera'. Translated from the Greek, kalitera means "the best." The

Origanum majorana, marjoram.

entire plant is gray to gray-green. The small, oval leaves are aromatically sweet, backed up by the sharp bite of Greek oregano, to which it is related.

Growing Tips Propagate 'Kalitera' from cuttings and root divisions. Keep plants free of weeds, and leave room around them for their fine-branching lateral roots. Severe, regular pruning keeps the plants attractive and bushy. Pinch or cut plants back before they flower. Harvest throughout the summer season as needed. Hardy in Zones 5 to 9.

Cultivars and Related Species The similarity in appearance and growing habits of marjoram and oregano has caused problems with identification for cooks and herbalists alike. Italian oregano (*Origanum* × *majoricum*, page 33), also known as Sicilian oregano or hardy marjoram, is a hybrid of sweet marjoram (*O. majorana*, page 56) and Greek oregano (*O. vulgare*). It has a more pronounced sweet aroma and less bitter flavor than Greek oregano, which has small, pointed, oval green leaves with a yellowish tinge and tastes pungent and bitter, like a blend of savory and thyme with a hint of pine, mint, and clove. Its small flowers range from purple to white and dry well for everlasting arrangements, but be aware that the plant roams freely and tends to take over.

Companion Plants Generous air and soil space, at least six inches around the plant, is best for this rare specimen. Sage planted nearby will echo its silver foliage.

Rosmarinus officinalis 'Salem' 'Salem' Rosemary

Rosmarinus officinalis 'Majorca Pink' 'Majorca Pink' Rosemary

'Salem', a favorite hardy rosemary variety, has a compact, many branched,

Origanum vulgare subsp. *hirtum* 'Kalitera', 'Kalitera' oregano.

erect habit and blue-violet flowers. The tender 'Majorca Pink' is a rowdy wonder. Its erect branches arch as they please and can be four feet tall. The leaves are stubby compared with those of other rosemary varieties. When in bloom, the lavender to pink flowers cover the green of the leaves in the most glorious way.

Growing Tips See *Rosmarinus officinalis*, page 35. For tips on overwintering rosemary indoors, see *Rosmarinus officinalis* 'Joyce DeBaggio', page 47. 'Salem' is hardy in Zones 6 to 10; 'Majorca Pink' in Zones 6 (with protection) to 9.

Cultivars and Related Species For hardy varieties, see *Rosmarinus officinalis*, page 35; for tender varieties, see *Rosmarinus officinalis*, 'Joyce DeBaggio', page 47. 'Huntington's Carpet', 'Golden Prostrate', 'Prostratus', and 'Santa Barbara'—which all appear to be different names for the same plant—lead the

Salvia officinalis 'Nana', 'Nana' sage.

rosemary collector on a confusing adventure. Nonetheless, if the plants hug their way down a wall as they grow, they can only be called gorgeous. Leaves are shiny green, and branches follow the contours of the land and containers in which they are planted.

Companion Plants Creeping thymes such as caraway thyme (*Thymus herba-barona*, page 23) and low mounds of sweet marjoram (*Origanum majorana*, page 56) are nice with both 'Salem' and 'Majora Pink' if kept at a safe distance and not allowed to touch the rosemary.

Salvia officinalis 'Nana'
'Nana' Sage

'Nana', a fine choice for a Mediterranean garden, has very small gray-green leaves and grows vigorously in a compact mound. It has proven tough and reliable in both frigid cold and steamy heat. In spring, blue flowers liberally cover the top of the plant.

Growing Tips See *Salvia officinalis* 'Woodcote Farm', page 48.

Cultivars and Related Species Common sage, *Salvia officinalis*, has purple- or blue-flowering spikes and grows two to three feet tall and three feet in diameter. Greek sage, *Salvia fruticosa* syn. *S. triloba,* an interesting plant that accounts for as much as 95 percent of the commercial dried sage sold in North America, has egg-shaped, furry gray leaves and blue flower spikes. Try these three cultivars as annual accents in the Mediterranean garden: 'Icterina', a diminutive bush with lavender-blue flowers and green leaves edged in gold; 'Purpurascens', which has wide, muted purple-and-green leaves with lavender-blue flowers; 'Tricolor', which has irregular blotches of green, white, and rose pink.

Companion Plants Sage's cultural requirements, as well as its leaf color and texture, make it a good companion for other Mediterranean plants. Also try grouping several varieties of sage together to make a magic carpet, leaving plenty of space between the plants.

Santolina chamaecyparissus
Gray Santolina

Santolina pinnata
Green Santolina

Easily pruned and shaped, both gray and green santolina have been used in knot gardens for centuries. This aromatic, evergreen shrub, also known as lavender cotton, has finely divided gray-green leaves and woolly white stems. Generally, these slow growers don't get much taller than two feet in height, and there are a number of dwarf varieties that stay even closer to the ground. Santolina grows in soft mounds and sends up stems with bright-yellow, button-shaped little flowers in summer. Green santolina is taller and brighter in color with thinner leaves that have a more feathery look. Gray santolina has denser, thicker leaves reminiscent of a carpet. It also stays more compact.

Growing Tips Sow santolina from seed, or layer in fall. The center of the clump tends to separate; prune plants back in the spring to help control this trait. In cold winters plants will die back, but

they'll send out new growth in spring. Hardy in Zones 6 to 8.

Cultivars and Related Species *Santolina chamaecyparissus* 'Lemon Queen' has cream-colored flowers and a sweet fragrance. 'Nana' is a low-growing dwarf variety that creates a thick groundcover. *Santolina virens* (also known as *S. viridis*) is a green-leafed santolina; *S. pinnata* subsp. *neapolitana*, one of the taller santolinas, has either green or gray feathery leaves.

Companion Plants German chamomile (*Matricaria recutita,* page TH), with golden flowers atop dark green foliage, complements the flowers and leaves of santolinas. Yellow-flowering plants like coreopsis and black-eyed Susan (*Rudbeckia*) make a good show behind green santolina (be sure to allow plenty of space for air circulation). The downy leaves of lamb's ears (*Stachys byzantina*) are a nice contrast to the coarse leaves of gray santolina.

Satureja montana • Winter Savory

Winter savory is a neglected herb not often used in North American gardens and kitchens—but once you grow it and use it, you'll be glad you did. This plant has erect stems, narrow, pointed, stiff leaves nearly an inch long, and a woody rootstock. It can become somewhat unruly but is easily shaped in the spring. If it is not trimmed, winter savory grows to about 18 inches tall. Flowers are white or very pale lavender, sometimes with darker purple spots. The leaves are darker green and much more peppery and stronger in flavor than those of summer savory (*Satureja hortensis*, page 22) and lack any sweetness. Winter savory plants are long-lived and dependable in dry and humid climates alike.

Santolina chamaecyparissus, gray santolina.

Growing Tips Start winter savory from seed in spring; divide or layer it in spring or fall. Take cuttings from soft new growth, not woody stems, in late spring or early summer. Space plants about a foot apart in neutral to slightly acid soil. Harvest regularly in spring; regular pruning will keep plants bushy and productive. Hardy in Zones 5 to 8.

Cultivars and Related Species Lemon savory (*Satureja biflora*, page 37) is great in the kitchen. Annual summer savory (*S. hortensis*, page 22) doesn't taste as sharp as winter savory; use it to flavor vinegar to splash on steamed green beans. Thyme-leafed savory (*S. thymbra*) is a tender perennial sporting clusters of pink flowers along stiff stems. Its leaves are stiff, somewhat bristly, and highly aromatic. Hardy in Zones 6 to 9.

Satureja montana, **winter savory.**

Companion Plants Winter savory serves nicely as an evergreen backdrop to more colorful plants outside the Mediterannean garden. Plant it as a border for a row of hyacinth beans (*Lablab purpureus*) or scarlet runner beans (*Phaseolus coccineus*). Other annuals with edible flowers such as signet marigold (*Tagetes tenuifolia*, page 111) and nasturtiums (*Tropaeolum*) may be used around winter savory to add pizzazz and culinary pleasure.

Thymus vulgaris 'Broadleaf English' 'Broadleaf English' Thyme

Tasty 'Broadleaf English', an erect-growing garden thyme selection, does not droop to the ground and so will be grit-free when you take it to the kitchen. This small, woody perennial has wide leaves with rounded margins and can range from 6 to 15 inches in height.

Growing Tips See *Thymus* × *citriodorus* 'Aureus', page 49. Thyme species germinate easily from seed, but cultivars tend

to be genetically unstable, and seed packets often contain a mixture of different seeds, so buy plant cultivars or propagate from cuttings. Hardy in Zones 4 to 8.

Cultivars and Related Species *Thymus* 'Argenteus' (page 71), silver thyme, is an attractive, low-spreading subshrub with silvery green leaves. The lemon thymes (*Thymus* × *citriodorus*) are handsome compact shrubs in a variety of colors from green to gold to variegated (*T.* × *citriodorus* 'Aureus', page 49) that provide the garden and kitchen with wonderful lemon fragrance and flavor. Tasty gray-leafed French thyme, *Thymus vulgaris* 'Narrow Leaf French' (page 112), works well as a pot or edging plant.

Companion Plants Rosemary (*Rosmarinus officinalis* and cultivars, pages 35, 47, 70), lavender (*Lavandula* species, hybrids, and cultivars, pages 55, 68), santolina (page 59), and related thymes go nicely with 'Broadleaf English' when planted at a polite distance.

Giving Your Soil a Mediterranean Twist

Climates and soils vary from garden to garden, and though you can't control the climate, you can alter the soil to create conditions similar to those around the Mediterranean and provide a healthy foundation for plant roots. If your soil is already alkaline, you will not need to use the oyster shell that is listed in the mixes below.

AGGREGATE MIX

This mix is rich in calcium and other minerals.

    Crushed oyster shell
    Activated charcoal
    Greensand (sandy rock or sediment
      high in glauconite)
    Granite meal

Combine one gallon of each ingredient in one of two five-gallon buckets. Pour the mixture from one bucket into the other a few times to make sure the ingredients blend well. Use 10 to 40 pounds per 100 square feet. Also amend the soil with compost or worm castings, which contain acids and beneficial bacteria that help the mineral elements in the aggregate mix dissolve over time. Use 5 to 20 pounds of worm castings or compost per 100 square feet of garden space. Use the aggregate mix when creating new beds or when planting new Mediterranean herbs in established conventional beds.

MEAL MIX

This is a balanced fertilizer that gives new plants a quick boost.

    Fish meal (10-2-2)
    Bone meal (5-12-0 plus 15% calcium)
    Kelp (variable N 1.7–2.5, P 5,
      K 2.25–6.25)

Combine equal parts fish, bone, and kelp in a one-gallon container. Blend well. Use three to nine pounds per 100 square feet. Add meal mix when preparing new beds and add two tablespoons or so to new plant holes.

MEDITERRANEAN MULCH

This mulch acts as a barrier between lower leaf surfaces and soil-dwelling fungal spores, cools the surface of the soil, and conserves moisture. It breaks down very slowly and looks attractive among plants in the Mediterranean garden.

    Crushed oyster shell
    Greensand
    Activated charcoal
    Coarse sand
    Granite or rock dust
    Lava rock

Combine the ingredients in equal parts. Apply to soil surface to one inch thick. The particles in the mulch will naturally differ in size and add to the pleasing texture of the mulch. Apply mulch after planting herbs in the garden or in pots, and replenish annually as needed.

WHERE TO FIND INGREDIENTS

Sand: builder's supply stores and garden centers

Compost and worm castings: home or local producer; composted cow manure at garden centers

Crushed oyster shell: farm-supply stores (the crushed shell is fed to chickens to produce hard-shelled eggs)

Lava rock: garden centers

Greensand, activated charcoal, granite meal, fish meal, kelp meal, and blood meal may be a bit more difficult to come by locally but can be ordered through organic gardening companies.

A Potted Herb Garden

Holly Shimizu

Herbs have long been favorite plants for container culture. For one thing, it's easy to harvest herbs as you're cooking when they're conveniently located in a pot near the kitchen door. In addition, herbs thrive in containers and add both zest and beauty to a moveable garden. They offer rich foliage colors and textures that can enhance a whole range of container styles. Best of all, containers are portable—they can be rotated, moved, used as architectural accents, and even hauled indoors for protection as needed.

Start your container herb garden with a large pot, roughly three feet in diameter at the top, so you'll have room to combine the plants in a pleasing design. In a large container, the plants have room to grow, slowly filling the available soil space. In a small pot, the roots eventually become root-bound, which stresses the plants.

The container should have drainage holes in the bottom so that excess water can escape; most herbs do not thrive in overly wet soil. Fill it with a good soil blend that contains one part sterilized compost and two parts commercial potting mix. Compost helps prevent the potting mix from drying out. Put the container on pot feet or place a gravel-filled tray underneath it, so it doesn't stand in water.

When you're ready to plant, make sure that the potting mix is moist but not wet. Set taller herbs in the center of the container and shorter plants toward the rim. If you want the pot to look full from the start, set the herbs close together. If you are patient and can

Continued on page 66

For maximum impact, group a large number of containers together, or as many as you have time and energy to care for. When matching plants to individual containers, bear in mind that small plants can look very attractive in tall pots and that tall plants are rather nice in squat pots.

A Potted Herb Garden

Whether you garden on a city patio or an expansive country estate, you can create a very effective herb garden by grouping together pots, tubs, and troughs of complementary shapes and sizes. Look for pots that fit your overall garden style, add a pleasant texture, and suit the needs of the herbs you want to grow. Choices include beautiful but frost-sensitive terra-cotta; winter-resistant cement; fiberglass and plastic, which are lightweight but can break down in the sun; and wood, which is naturally handsome but heavy and rot-prone. Containers need not be round—in fact, square or rectangular containers are less likely to blow over in heavy winds. As you choose plants for your container garden, imagine the herbs growing abundantly into an exuberant bouquet of texture, color, and fragrance. Two striking container combinations are illustrated in the illustration above. Herbs suitable for growing in containers are described beginning on page 67.

Design Tips

- To achieve rich textural contrasts, select plants that offer variations in foliage and color from bold to delicate, in shapes from upright to spiky or trailing.

- For a season of continuous drama, combine herbs that flower at different times.

- Choosing annual, biennial, and perennial herbs with their different life cycles will ensure that something new is always going on in your potted garden.

- Soften the edges of your containers with an elegantly trailing herbal ground cover such as caraway thyme (*Thymus herba-barona*) or golden oregano (*Origanum vulgare* 'Aureum').

Plants Featured in This Garden

1 *Calamintha nepeta*, lesser calamint

2 *Lavandula multifida*, fernleaf lavender

3 *Matricaria recutita*, German chamomile

4 *Mentha* × *gracilis*, doublemint

5 *Ocimum basilicum*, sweet basil

6 *Ocimum basilicum* 'Minimum Purpureum', miniature purple basil

7 *Plectranthus amboinicus,* Cuban oregano

8 *Rosmarinus officinalis* 'Tuscan Blue', 'Tuscan Blue' rosemary

9 *Thymus* 'Argenteus', silver thyme

10 *Thymus* × *citriodorus* 'Aureus', lemon thyme

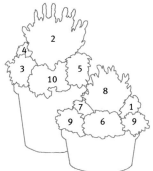

Make the most of the great variation of plant forms and foliage textures when placing your containers. Group the herbs so that trailing plants complement mounding and taller herbs. Set off bold leaf shapes with delicate foliage. Add some color with herbs that flower at different times.

plan for the long term, spread the plants farther apart and wait for them to fill out. Once you've planted your herbs, water them in until water runs out through the holes in the bottom of the container. Containers dry out quickly, so check yours frequently, as young plants are sensitive to drying out—but be careful not to overwater, either. Turn the pot if necessary to give all plants equal access to the sun and keep their growth evenly distributed. Most herbs will develop bushier growth and a fuller appearance if you pinch back new growth as it emerges. When you start to see growth, fertilize the container every two to three weeks, but curtail fertilizer applications toward the end of summer. An organic fertilizer of kelp and fish emulsion gives excellent results. Harvest herbs and cut them back as needed throughout the summer.

Herbs need direct sunlight to achieve their maximum flavor and fragrance, so place your potted herbs where they will receive at least six hours of direct sunlight. In shade, most herbs become leggy and lack intense flavor.

Herbs for a Potted Garden

Calamintha nepeta
Lesser Calamint

Lesser calamint adds a delicate texture, fine pale pink flowers, and a minty fragrance to your container. It has a showy form like baby's breath (*Gypsophila*) and contrasts well with bolder and coarser herbs. Plants grow 24 to 30 inches tall. Lesser calamint's extended blooming period in mid- to late summer will help fill out the container and give it an abundant, overflowing appearance. Use the leaves for tea, potpourri, or as a flavoring with mushrooms.

Growing Tips Lesser calamint grows easily from seed or can be propagated by cuttings. It prefers sun but will tolerate light shade. Hardy in Zones 5 to 9.

Cultivars and Related Species Look for closely related herbs in the mint family that aren't as aggressive as the more common spearmint (*Mentha spicata*) and peppermint (*M.* × *piperita*). Large-flowered calamint, or showy savory (*Calamintha grandiflora*), is a taller, more robust relative. Alpine calamint (*Acinos alpinus*) is an excellent closely related low-growing perennial with gray leaves and blue-purple flowers that grows well in a rock garden.

Companion Plants Lesser calamint looks great with bold-textured herbs such as scented geraniums (*Pelargonium tomentosum*, page 69; *Pelargonium* cultivars, page 19) and Cuban oregano (*Plectranthus amboinicus*, page 69).

Foeniculum vulgare 'Rubrum'
'Rubrum' Bronze Fennel

The finely dissected, maroon leaves of bronze fennel have a feathery texture and reach a height of about two feet. The fragrant leaves add a delicate

Calamintha nepeta, lesser calamint.

licorice flavor to foods such as fish, and the seeds make a wonderful tea or flavoring. Yellow umbel flowers bloom beautifully in late summer, adding to this herb's magnificence; use them in cut-flower arrangements.

Growing Tips Bronze fennel is easy to grow from seed, and it reseeds itself vigorously. To avoid rampant volunteers, remove seedheads before they ripen. Grow this short-lived perennial as an annual in colder regions. Hardy in Zones 7 to 10.

Cultivars and Related Species The closely related sweet green fennel (*Foeniculum vulgare* var. *dulce*) differs from bronze fennel only in its green leaf color. The vegetable called fennel, also known as finnochio (*Foeniculum vulgare* var. *azoricum*) is another close relative. It has an enlarged bulbous base and belongs in the vegetable garden.

Companion Plants This bronze plant looks best with gray foliage such as that of silver thyme (*Thymus* 'Argenteus', 71) or artichoke (*Cynara scolymus*).

Lavandula multifida
Fernleaf Lavender

The finely dissected gray leaves of this lavender provide lovely texture and a camphorlike fragrance, and its abundant spikes of true blue-lavender flowers can reach to three inches. Fernleaf lavender will bloom all summer.

Growing Tips Fernleaf lavender is easily grown from seed or cuttings. You can increase blooms by deadheading plants. This herb distinguishes itself from its relatives by its long blooming season and lack of hardiness. Overwinter it indoors in cooler climates by giving it lots of light and not too much water. Hardy in Zones 9 to 10.

Cultivars and Related Species All lavender species and hybrids are good for growing in pots. For some more suggestions, see *Lavandula angustifolia* 'Royal Velvet', page 55, and *Lavandula × intermedia* 'Grosso', page 55.

Companion Plants Fernleaf lavender is beautiful in combination with Mexican tarragon (*Tagetes lucida*, page 70), basils (*Ocimum* cultivars, pages 18, 32, 46, 68), or thymes (*Thymus* species and cultivars, pages 23, 49, 60, 71, 112).

Ocimum basilicum 'Minimum Purpureum'
Miniature Purple Basil

This basil's abundant small, rich purple-burgundy leaves form mounds that can fall gracefully over the container edge and, if well placed, help create a rhythm of contrasting textures. Plants grow from 6 to 12 inches tall. Clip the leaves throughout the growing season for use in vinegars, salads, and sauces.

Growing Tips Propagate 'Minimum Purpureum' from cuttings in a warm greenhouse. Basil loves hot weather and tolerates no frost.

Lavandula multifida, fernleaf lavender, at right.

Cultivars and Related Species *Ocimum basilicum* 'Dark Opal' is similar in color but has much larger leaves. Miniature green-leafed cultivars are also available. 'Spicy Globe' is a freely branching compact plant with a rounded growth habit, as is 'Minimum', page 18.

Companion Plants For a stunning contrast, place miniature purple basil next to golden lemon thyme (*Thymus* × *citriodorus* 'Doone Valley' or 'Aureus', page 49) along the edge of a container.

Pelargonium tomentosum
Peppermint-Scented Geranium

Scented pelargoniums are a reliable group of wonderful plants, native to South Africa, that offer fragrances from chocolate to apple to mint, with hundreds of variations. One of the most textural is the peppermint-scented geranium, with gray, velvety leaves that are richly scented of peppermint. Plants grow from one to two feet tall and spread horizonally as well.

Growing Tips Place this vigorous grower at the edge of a container to spill over and soften the rim; prune it back if its growth is too exuberant. Peppermint-scented geranium tolerates no frost. Propagate it from softwood cuttings taken in late summer and late winter. They will root easily and make lovely houseplants in winter. Hardy in Zones 10 to 11.

Cultivars and Related Species See *Pelargonium* 'Charity' and 'Poquito', page 19.

Companion Plants Peppermint-scented geranium's silvery velvet leaves look superb with the feathery leaves of bronze fennel (*Foeniculum vulgare* 'Rubrum', page 67) or the flowering spikes of lavender (*Lavandula* species, hybrids, and cultivars, pages 55, 68, 109).

Plectranthus amboinicus
Cuban Oregano

The succulent velvety leaves of Cuban oregano have scalloped edges and are prized for their zippy oregano flavor. This herb is better known in hot climates, where cooks use it in bean dishes and with shellfish. Plants grow from 12 to 18 inches tall and have succulent, furry bright green leaves.

Growing Tips Plants are easily propagated by cuttings. This tender perennial does not tolerate frost. Move it indoors and place it under lights for winter. Hardy in Zones 10 and 11.

Cultivars and Related Species A closely related variegated form, *Plectranthus amboinicus* 'Variegatus', is highly ornamental and has a similar distinctive flavor.

Companion Plants Cuban oregano grows well in hanging baskets or pots with upright plants such as basils (*Ocimum*

basilicum cultivars, pages 18, 32, 68) and lavenders (*Lavandula* species, hybrids, and cultivars, pages 55, 68, 109).

Rosmarinus officinalis 'Tuscan Blue'
'Tuscan Blue' Rosemary

The tall, spiky, gray-green leaves of rosemary are an excellent foil for the center of a container, surrounded by other herbs. Many cultivars are available, but the most attractive selection for container culture is known as 'Tuscan Blue'. It has large, abundant leaves and a full form and will grow from one to three feet tall (taller in warmer climates). Rosemary's piney flavor and fragrance is useful in aromatherapy, cooking, and wreath making.

Growing Tips and Cultivars and Related Species Propagate rosemary by cuttings. See also *Rosmarinus officinalis,* page 35. For information on overwintering indoors, see *Rosmarinus officinalis* 'Joyce DeBaggio', page 47. Hardy in Zones 7 to 10.

Companion Plants Grow rosemary to complement round-leafed herbs such as Cuban oregano (*Plectranthus amboinicus*, page 69) and fine-textured plants like calamint (*Calamintha nepeta*, page 67).

Tagetes lucida • Mexican Tarragon

In southern climates gardeners grow this tender perennial treated as an annual instead of French tarragon (*Artemisia dracunculus*) to give their dishes a sweet anise flavor. Both flowers and leaves can add a spark to salads, vegetables, and fish. Toward the end of summer its bright yellow flowers add zest to a container herb garden. Plants grow from 18 to 24 inches tall, with handsome linear leaves and an upright form.

Growing Tips To propagate Mexican tarragon, take cuttings before flowers appear. Overwinter rooted cuttings indoors under lights. Hardy in Zones 8 to 10.

Cultivars and Related Species *Tagetes tenuifolia* 'Tangerine Gem' has more

Tagetes lucida, Mexican tarragon.

Thymus 'Argenteus', silver thyme.

orange color; 'Lulu' is a dwarf cultivar. 'Lemon Gem' is on page 111.

Companion Plants Mexican tarragon looks good with the spiky gray-green foliage of lavender (*Lavandula* species, hybrids, and cultivars, pages 55, 68, 109) or combined with basils (*Ocimum basilicum* cultivars, pages 18, 32, 68), which are also fond of heat. Or try combining it with with nasturtiums (*Tropaeolum*) or with Texas sage (*Salvia coccinea* 'Lady in Red').

Thymus 'Argenteus'
Silver Thyme

The attractive gray-green leaves of this thyme are edged with the barest line of white and have a unique silver glow. This low-spreading shrub or subshrub flowers in pale blue and shows a tinge of pink in cold weather. Silver thyme forms an aromatic mound and makes an eye-catching border. Plants grow to 12 inches tall.

Growing Tips See *Thymus* × *citriodorus* 'Aureus', page 49. 'Argenteus' is best propagated by cuttings taken in summer. Hardy in Zones 7 to 9.

Cultivars and Related Species Both *Thymus vulgaris* 'Broadleaf English' (page 60) and 'Narrowleaf French' (page 112) are especially good for cooking. For citrusy scents, try *Thymus vulgaris* 'Orange Balsam'; lemon thyme (*T.* × *citriodorus*); golden lemon thyme (*T.* × *citriodorus* 'Aureus', page 49), which has beautiful golden leaves; and *T.* × *citriodorus* 'Silver Queen', which has silver-edged foliage.

Companion Plants Low-growing silver thyme is great in front of basils (*Ocimum basilicum* cultivars, pages 18, 32, 68), lavenders (*Lavandula* species, hybrids, and cultivars, pages 55, 68, 109), and rosemary (*Rosmarinus officinalis* and cultivars, pages 35, 47, 57, 70).

A Garden of Shade-Loving Herbs

Holly Shimizu

Though it is true that most herbs prefer full sun, there are some that thrive in shade or require at least some shade for their best performance. Gardening with herbs in the shade can be an excellent retreat from the sun. The exact amount of shade a particular herb needs or tolerates depends on the intensity of the summer sun and varies depending on the region. Numerous herbs can grow in the sun in the North but need protection from the intense light in southern areas in the summer.

To assess the intensity and duration of shade, horticulturists have come up with a few simple terms to qualify it. An area is in partial shade or light shade when it receives a minimum of six hours of direct sunlight, but at least four of them are in the morning when the sun is less intense. In filtered or dappled shade some sunlight is blocked by overhead trees or structures such as lattices. In full or dense shade, there is no direct sunlight. With the exception of wildflowers that bloom before leaves fully develop on overhead trees, few plants can thrive in dense shade unless they receive ambient or reflected sunlight.

To encourage plant growth in the shade of trees, consider pruning some lower branches to let in light and improve air circulation. Be sure not to destroy the elegance and grace of the trees while opening up the garden for layers of underplanting.

Continued on page 76

Offering respite from the sun, a garden in the shade is an invitation to linger. Site North American native *Asarum canadense*, wild ginger, near a path to allow close scrutiny of its unusual flowers.

Shade Garden

Creating an herb garden in areas with less than full sun provides opportunities to blend the herbs with other plants in different landscape styles, from a shady border to a woodland garden. The single most important factor in choosing which herbs to grow is selecting those suited to the light levels on your site (see page 73). The foremost design consideration is to combine herbs with contrasting habits and textures. Angelica (*Angelica archangelica*), for example, is a statuesque plant in any setting. Sweet cicely (*Myrrhis odorata*) has a soft, fine, ferny texture. Set these off with plants with sharply vertical leaves, such as mioga ginger (*Zingiber mioga*) or shade-loving irises. If winter interest is important, blend in evergreens like hellebores or epimediums. Don't feel obliged to blend herbs only with herbs. They are at home with many other types of shade-loving plants, including ferns and woodland wildflowers from foamflower (*Tiarella cordifolia*) to columbines (*Aquilegia*) to phlox. For additional recommendations, see pages 77 to 85.

Growing Tips

• Most shade-loving plants, herbs included, are woodland denizens that prefer a consistently moist (but not soggy), humus-rich soil.

• Before sowing seed or planting, amend poor soils with compost or other organic matter.

• Transplant herbs before or after periods of active growth when the plants can devote more energy to settling in and becoming established.

• To conserve water and keep the garden evenly moist, mulch with several inches of compost, leaf mold, well-rotted manure, or shredded bark.

Plants Featured in This Garden

1 *Angelica archangelica*, angelica

2 *Asarum canadense*, wild ginger

3 *Galium odoratum*, sweet woodruff

4 *Hedeoma pulegioides*, American pennyroyal

5 *Hierochloe odorata*, holy grass

6 *Myrrhis odorata*, sweet cicely

7 *Zingiber mioga*, mioga ginger

Most herbs need abundant sunshine to do well, but there are some that require at least some shade. Wild ginger, *Asarum canadense*, mingling here with common maidenhair fern, *Adiantum capillus-veneris*, is native to moist woodlands and thrives in a shady garden.

The trees' roots may also compete with those of the herbaceous plants for nutrients and water. Many plants cannot thrive around shallow-rooted trees such as beeches (*Fagus*), red maple (*Acer rubrum*), sugar maple (*A. saccharum*), and birches (*Betula*) because the trees' abundant root systems take up most of the surface water. Herbaceous plants may grow more easily around trees such as oaks (*Quercus*), which typically send most of their roots downward rather than out to take up water. In any case, you can carefully prune some of the trees' fine hair roots with a sharp spade or a pruning saw. This will give your herbs room to grow for several years until the trees have grown new roots and you have to prune again.

Herbs for a Shade Garden

Angelica archangelica
Angelica

This statuesque short-lived perennial, often grown as a biennial, reaches two to five feet tall and often three feet across. In its second year angelica produces six-inch round flower heads with whitish-green starry flowers atop thick, ribbed, succulent stems tinged with purple. The fragrant flowers attract many good insects, including honeybees and beneficial wasps. Angelica's fresh leaves are used to sweeten acidic fruits such as rhubarb; its stems are candied as a sweet; and its seeds are added to pastries. A few cautions: Eat angelica only in small amounts, since it may be carcinogenic. Because it contains furanocoumarins, handling angelica can heighten the skin's sensitivity to sunlight. In addition, angelica closely resembles one of its poisonous cousins, poison hemlock (*Conium maculatum*), which has more finely divided feathery leaves.

Growing Tips Hot-climate gardeners must grow angelica in some shade or the summer sun will bake it. Cold-climate gardeners can grow it in the sun. The soil should be rich and moist yet well drained with plenty of organic matter. Plants usually die after blooming in their second year, but if you scatter the seeds in place, they will often germinate. Grow seeds when they are fresh, or freeze them in a moist soil medium until sowing. They stay viable for several years. Typical of plants in the carrot family, angelica has a taproot, so transplant with care in cool weather. Hardy in Zones 4 to 8.

Cultivars and Related Species Korean angelica (*Angelica gigas*) is a medicinal species with gorgeous burgundy flowers; purplestem angelica (*A. atropurpurea*) is a

Angelica archangelica, angelica.

native species found in swamps and moist woods in eastern Canada and the U.S.

Companion Plants Angelica grows well in a shady border with perennials including hellebores, lily-of-the-valley (*Convallaria majalis*, page 92), sweet woodruff (*Galium odoratum*, page 80), epimediums, and ferns.

Anthriscus cerefolium • Chervil

Chervil is a mounding short-lived annual herb with finely dissected leaves that have a wispy, ferny texture; it reaches a height of one to two feet. Best known for its association with French cuisine, it is one of the ingredients in the *fines herbes* blends often used to flavor eggs, fish, and salads. Its delightful flavor is described as resembling anise. After blooming, the beautiful white umbel flower heads form dark brown seeds. Chervil closely resembles the perennial shade-loving herb sweet cicely (*Myrrhis odorata*, page 84).

Cryptotaenia japonica, **mitsuba.**

Growing Tips Chervil grows well in rich, moist soils in cool shade. Where summers are cool, chervil does well in full sun. Grow it from seed in early spring or in late summer for a harvestable crop of leaves in four to six weeks. For successive harvests, sow seeds at regular intervals during spring and late summer. In warm areas chervil will not thrive during the heat of summer, but you can seed it in fall for a winter garden. Chervil is a true annual.

Cultivars and Related Species Chervil is in the carrot family (also known as the umbel family) and related to sun-loving dill, coriander, parsley, and fennel, as well as shade-loving sweet cicely (*Myrrhis odorata*, page 84).

Companion Plants Chervil looks wonderful edging a shady path. It's also lovely in a container, where you might try combining it with herbs that emerge later in the season, such as chives (*Allium schoenoprasum*).

Asarum canadense
Wild Ginger

This native herbaceous perennial, well loved for its sparkling green, heart-shaped leaves, makes an excellent groundcover in shade. The brownish-red tubular flowers hide beneath the leaves. In the wild the plant is found in moist, rich woods in northeastern North America. Its creeping rhizomes are used as a flavoring, with a taste similar to ginger.

Growing Tips A hardy perennial that thrives in woodland-garden conditions with moist soils, wild ginger's growth is so thick that it can be an excellent weed suppressant. Although it can be grown from seed, it's best propagated by division. Hardy in Zones 4 to 8.

Cultivars and Related Species Among the many botanically interesting species in the genus is European ginger, *Asarum europaeum*, a gorgeous evergreen species with shiny green leaves that reach five to ten inches tall, hardy in Zones 4 to 7.

Companion Plants Grow wild ginger as an edging plant along a shady walkway or as a groundcover. It blends well with ferns, hostas, and other shade herbs, such as sweet cicely (*Myrrhis odorata*, page 84).

Cryptotaenia japonica
Mitsuba, Japanese Wild Parsley

This short-lived perennial herb is grown and used extensively in Japan, where it is known as mitsuba ("three leaves"), a name that refers to its three-part, doubly serrated, dark green leaves. It grows approximately two feet tall and has insignificant small white flowers. Mitsuba is both an important culinary herb, used for its parsley-celery flavor, and an attractive ornamental plant. It looks a bit like flat-leaf parsley (*Petroselinum crispum* var. *neapolitanum*) but in flavor is more like chervil (*Anthriscus cerefolium*). Both its young spring leaves and young stems are harvested; older leaves tend to be bitter. It is excellent in salads and soups and with vegetables, eggs, and seafood.

Growing Tips Mitsuba is usually grown as an annual from seed, sometimes as a perennial. Grow it in rich, moist soil in shade; in cooler climates, it will tolerate some sun. Successive seed sowing is useful for regular harvest of young leaves. It often reseeds itself in place. Hardy in Zones 4 to 9.

Cultivars and Related Species *Cryptotaenia japonica* forma *atropurpurea* is grown for its very attractive purple leaves; *C. canadensis* is a species native to the piedmont forests of eastern North America. These two are nice in the garden, but mitsuba is best for eating.

Companion Plants In cooler climates, mitsuba grows successfully in a sunny border with other herbs such as bee balm (*Monarda didyma*, page 45), and it pairs nicely in the shade with sweet violets (*Viola odorata*, page 98), chervil (*Anthriscus cerefolium*, page 77), or musk geranium (*Geranium macrorhizum*, page 80). It's also at home in a cool-climate vegetable garden, where it can be used as an attractive border or edging plant.

Cunila origanoides
Maryland Dittany, Stone Mint

In the wild this small and little-known member of the mint family is found on stony outcroppings in eastern North America. It grows from 12 to 18 inches tall with slightly toothed leaves and sweet purple-pink and sometimes white flowers, which appear toward the end of summer. The mint-marjoram-scented leaves are used as a flavorful tea, and the flowers are pretty in dried arrangements.

Growing Tips Maryland dittany prefers a well-drained but moist site with good organic matter in a slightly acidic soil in partial shade. It's easy to grow from seed or division. Hardy in Zones 6 to 8.

Cultivars and Related Species Corsican mint (*Mentha requieni*, page 83) is a ground-hugging shade lover; American pennyroyal (*Hedeoma pulegioides*, page 81) grows more upright but also thrives in shade. Doublemint (*Mentha* × *gracilis* 'Madalene Hill', page 31) and orange mint (*Mentha aquatica*, page 44) are popular for cooking and teas, but they prefer sunny spots to shade and are rather aggressive.

Cunila origanoides, **Maryland dittany.**

Companion Plants Maryland dittany is not an aggressive mint and looks at home with sweet woodruff (*Galium odoratum*, page SH) and wild ginger (*Asarum canadense*, page SH). It also thrives in the nooks and crannies of a shady rock garden or along a woodland path.

Galium odoratum
Sweet Woodruff

This lovely herbal groundcover has bright green, whorled, pointed leaves and small, white, star-shaped flowers. Rounded, sticky seeds sit atop square stems. A herbaceous perennial, sweet woodruff grows roughly 6 to 12 inches high and creeps along the ground. Its leaves contain coumarin, which makes them smell like freshly cut hay or vanilla when dry. Traditionally, the leaves are used to add flavor to May wine, as a wonderfully fragrant ingredient in pot pourri, or as a strewing herb in churches.

Sweet woodruff, *Galium odoratum.*

Growing Tips Native to European woodlands, sweet woodruff prefers a shady spot in rich, evenly moist soil. If happy in its location, it will spread quickly; it can be controlled by division or by confinement in a container. It is most easily propagated by division. Hardy in Zones 4 to 8.

Cultivars and Related Species Yellow bedstraw (*Galium verum*), an ancient herb that was once used for stuffing mattresses, is closely related, but it prefers to grow in sun and can be rather aggressive.

Companion Plants Sweet woodruff grows well under the shade of trees and looks great with hellebores, ferns, sweet cicely (*Myrrhis odorata*, page 84), and woodland wildflowers.

Geranium macrorhizum
Musk Geranium

Do not confuse this herb with the tender, fragrant geraniums that belong to the genus *Pelargonium*. Musk geranium is an aromatic, hardy herbaceous

Geranium macrorhizum 'Album', 'Album' musk geranium.

perennial that grows 15 to 18 inches tall and is semievergreen with gray-green, deeply divided, lobed leaves. Pink flowers appear abundantly above the velvety-textured leaves. Musk geranium is most valued for its distinctive, warm musky fragrance, hence its use in perfumery and in pot pourri.

Growing Tips Musk geranium is happiest in a woodland garden with shade or partial shade but is tolerant of dry shade. Grow it in soil rich in organic matter and divide it often. The plant has a long, sticky rhizome that starts above ground. Hardy in Zones 4 to 9.

Cultivars and Related Species Quite a few ornamental cultivars are available, including *Geranium macrorhizum* 'Album', with white flowers; 'Bevan's Variety', with magenta flowers; and 'Ingwersen's Variety', with light pink flowers and light green foliage.

Companion Plants Musk geranium grows well with epimediums, native grasses such as holy grass (*Hierochloe odorata*, page 82), or as a groundcover under the light shade of trees.

Hedeoma pulegioides
American Pennyroyal

This strongly scented native annual mint reaches a height of 10 to 12 inches, with branching stems, slightly hairy, toothed leaves, and bluish, tubular flowers that project from hairy green cups in the leaf axils. Pennyroyal was historically used as a medicinal tea but is not recommended currently for safety reasons, as it can be poisonous if ingested in large doses. Its leaves are most valuable for keeping away mosquitoes: Crush the leaves and rub them directly on the skin, or place them in alcohol to make an antimosquito spray. American pennyroyal smells much like English pennyroyal (*Mentha pulegium*); both have essential oils high in pulegone.

Hierochloe odorata, holy grass.

Growing Tips Easily grown from seed in good garden loam, American pennyroyal will reseed itself if conditions are right. In the central and eastern U.S. it can be found in woodlands and disturbed sites. It is an annual that can withstand light frost.

Cultivars and Related Species Other species of fragrant *Hedeoma* are found in parts of North and South America, but none are shade-tolerant. The genus *Hedeoma* is closely related to other mints, especially English pennyroyal (*Mentha pulegium*).

Companion Plants The slightly fuzzy foliage of American pennyroyal provides a nice contrast with may apple (*Podophyllum peltatum*, page 95), lily-of-the-valley (*Convallaria majalis,* page 92), or bee balm (*Monarda didyma*, page 45).

Hierochloe odorata
Holy Grass, Sweet Grass

One common name of this aromatic, grassy herb reflects its status as a sacred plant by Native Americans, who use it in purification ceremonies; its other name describes the enticing aroma it gives off when dry. Its scent of vanilla or newly mown hay arises from its principal component, coumarin. The herb's tufts of bright green leaves spread into mats and reach a height of about a foot. Its linear, flat, ⅛-inch-wide leaves are woven into baskets, mats, and incense ropes. The herb is used in Europe for strewing on church floors and as a flavoring in vodka to make *zubrowka*.

Growing Tips Holy grass is best grown from plugs or divisions planted in spring. It prefers moist, well-drained soil in light shade. This plant can be aggressive, so consider confining it to a container. Harvest the leaves in summer and dry them for maximum fragrance. Hardy in Zones 4 to 9.

Cultivars and Related Species Holy grass is closely related to sun-loving sweet vernal grass (*Anthoxanthum odoratum*), which also smells like newly mown hay when dry.

Companion Plants Holy grass can be mistaken for a weed because of its resemblance to other grasses. Try growing it in a container to make it stand out. It's also handsome combined with other small herbs such as American pennyroyal (*Hedeoma pulegioides*, page 81) or sweet woodruff (*Galium odoratum*, page 80).

Mentha requienii
Corsican Mint

This choice, tiny mint is a groundcover for moist shade. Compact, rounded leaves make this mint look much like baby's tears (*Soleirolia soleirolii*), although it is easily distinguished by its strong minty fragrance, reminiscent of the liqueur crème-de-menthe. Small purple flowers appear from the axils of the leaves.

Growing Tips Corsican mint grows easily from division. Plant it in a rich, moist soil, and don't allow it to dry out. It doesn't compete well with aggressive plants, so give it space along a walk, stream, or in a container for easy access to the leaves' pleasing aroma. Cover the plant lightly with pine needles in winter, or overwinter it indoors. Hardy in Zones 8 (7 with protection) to 9.

Cultivars and Related Species Closely related to other mints, Corsican mint is distinguished by its growth habit.

Companion Plants Corsican mint may be grown either in a container or as a shady groundcover if protected from more aggressive plants.

Monarda fistulosa
Wild Bergamot

An excellent native plant for a wild garden, *Monarda fistulosa* grows to two to three feet and has tousled pink-purple flowers that attract hummingbirds and bees. The square stems are hairy and branched, with slightly hairy lance-shaped leaves. Leaves and flowers are used to make an excellent tea, either hot or cold.

Growing Tips Wild bergamot likes partial shade in rich, well-drained soil—it's prone to mildew if grown in dry soil. If the leaves get mildew, cut the stems back to the base for rejuvenation. Hardy in Zones 4 to 10.

Monarda fistulosa, wild bergamot.

Cultivars and Related Species Many hybrids exist because of natural crosses between *Monarda fistulosa* and *M. didyma* (page 45). *Monarda fistulosa* is most commonly found in eastern North America. An interesting clone that originated in Manitoba, Canada, is high in geraniol, which gives it a rose scent. It is sold as *M. fistulosa* 'Rose' or 'Sweet'. *M. menthifolia* is found in the West.

Companion Plants Plant wild bergamot with wildflowers such as mayapples (*Podophyllum peltatum* (page 95), wild ginger (*Asarum canadense*, page 78), or columbines (*Aquilegia*).

Myrrhis odorata
Sweet Cicely

This soft-textured, ferny, mounding perennial herb is a delight in the shade garden. Whether it's tucked into a shady corner, set along a pathway, or even used as a low feathery accent plant, it is cherished for its beauty, aroma, and usefulness. The finely cut leaves resemble fern fronds, while its flat clusters of carrotlike tiny white flowers reach up to three inches across. Stems are hollow and slightly hairy. All parts of sweet cicely are aromatic and have a flavor and scent of sweet anise with a touch of celery. Fresh leaves and seed are used for their sweet taste in fruit dishes or baked products. The sticky, dark brown seeds are a good breath freshener. Sweet cicely's roots are sometimes cooked and eaten as a vegetable.

Growing Tips Like most of its relatives in the carrot family, this cool-weather-loving perennial has a taproot, so it resents transplanting. Grow it from fresh seed, or scatter seeds that are just falling off the plant on the ground, and new plants will come up on their own. Otherwise, collect the seed and place it in a moist soil medium and keep cool in the refrigerator. After approximately two months they will be ready to grow in humusy, moist soil. Hardy in Zones 5 to 8.

Cultivars and Related Species Do not confuse *Myrrhis odorata* with a native American woodland plant also called sweet cicely (*Osmorhiza*); both have fragrant, segmented leaves.

Companion Plants Sweet cicely looks great in a shady herb garden with sweet woodruff (*Galium odoratum*, page 80), wild ginger (*Asarum canadense*, page 78), musk geranium (*Geranium macrorhizum*, page 80), and wild bergamot (*Monarda fistulosa*, page 83).

Myrrhis odorata, **sweet cicely.**

Zingiber mioga, **mioga ginger.**

Zingiber mioga
Mioga Ginger

This Japanese native is known to many gardeners as hardy ginger due to its ability to thrive as a perennial in colder regions. Its gingerlike leaves have a tropical appearance, with medium green blades reaching two to three feet. The flowers are small, yellowish, basal spikes appearing in late summer or autumn; these are harvested for use in salads, as a flavoring with sushi, or pickled in vinegar for year-round use. Their taste is refreshing, with a gingery bite. Look for recipes using mioga ginger in Japanese cookbooks.

Growing Tips For best results, grow mioga ginger in very rich, very moist soil. Propagate it by division almost any time. Hardy in Zones 7 to 10 (Zone 6 with protection).

Cultivars and Related Species The fleshy rhizome of true ginger (*Zingiber officinale*) is routinely used in Asian foods, and though true ginger is less hardy in the garden than mioga ginger, its rhizomes are easily available in the grocery store.

Companion Plants If happy, this plant will grow vigorously, so plant it with other vigorous herbs that like moist conditions such as bee balm (*Monarda didyma*, page 45), mitsuba (*Cryptotaenia japonica*, page 79), or angelica (*Angelica archangelica*, page 77).

A Garden of Fragrant Herbs

Scott D. Appell

Gardeners everywhere can steal a page from my neighbors on the small Caribbean island of Vieques, southeast of Puerto Rico. Every household garden on the island contains a selection of fragrant, often medicinal herbs. Sour oranges and Caribbean, or key, limes are ubiquitous: Their perfumed flowers fill vases that adorn the dining table and bathroom, and the bitter fruits are used in everything from acne medications to cough syrups, and of course, food. Other fragrant tropical and subtropical medicinal herbs abound, including the spectacularly flowered queen of the night (*Selenicereus grandiflora*), a passionflower known as parcha (*Passiflora edulis*), Cuban oregano (*Plectranthus amboinicus*), rosemary (*Rosmarinus officinalis*), basil (*Ocimum basilicum* cultivars), Indian fig or prickly pear cactus (*Opuntia ficus-indica*), and aloes. But you don't have to live on a tropical island paradise to appreciate plants like these. They, along with fragrant species native to temperate climates, can add an intoxicating dimension to gardens anywhere.

I developed a fascination with fragrant herbs as a youngster. What made these plants smell so good? Why did their scents linger on my fingertips until I thoroughly scrubbed my hands? The fragrances of scented geraniums (*Pelargonium*), mints (*Mentha* species and cultivars), bee balms (*Monarda*), sages (*Salvia*), and thymes (*Thymus*), to name a scant few, arise from the volatile water- (and insect-) repellent

Continued on page 90

Be sure to place a bench or other seat near fragrant herbs such as lily-of-the-valley, *Convallaria majalis*, a true harbinger of spring, so you can linger and appreciate their perfume.

A Garden of Fragrant Herbs

In a garden of fragrant herbs, proximity is all-important. Most scented herbs are aromatic only when the foliage is rubbed, brushed, or bruised to release its essential oils. A seat or bench is an invitation to sit and linger, catch perfumes on the breeze, or gently caress a leaf or bloom. If one seat is not enough, arrange several benches in strategic spots throughout the garden, as in the landscape plan above. You can also make fragrant herbs more accessible by elevating your garden with raised beds and wall or arbor plantings, or by simply hoisting potted herbs onto sturdy stands. Still another option is to fill a footed urn or other tall decorative container with fragrant herbs such as those showcased on pages 91 to 99—a great focal point that will be greatly appreciated by you and your guests, who won't have to bow or stoop to take in the botanical perfumes.

Design Tips

- Enjoy your fragrant herbs 24/7—surround your sitting area with evening-scented herbs such as angel's trumpet (*Datura inoxia*) and night-scented stock (*Matthiola longipetala*) and you're sure to become a night owl.

- Put a very low seat in your fragrance garden, about eight inches high, to better appreciate the perfumes of short-statured plants like sweet violet (*Viola odorata*) and lily-of-the-valley (*Convallaria majalis*).

- Children will love their own tiny bench to help get their hands and noses close to fuzzy, fragrant plants.

- For especially tall fragrant herbs like late-season lilies (*Lilium orientalis*, *L. aureum*), you'll need a different plan of action: a small stepladder fashioned from flagstones or wood, or a sturdy wooden ladder placed up against such stately plants.

Plants Featured in This Garden

1 *Acorus calamus*, calamus

2 *Citrus* species, citrus

3 *Convallaria majalis*, lily-of-the-valley

4 *Iris pallida*, orris root

5 *Melissa officinalis* 'Aurea', variegated lemon balm

6 *Passiflora incarnata*, maypop

7 *Podophyllum peltatum*, may apple

8 *Pogostemon cablin*, patchouli

9 *Sassafras albidum*, sassafras

10 *Selenicereus grandiflorus*, queen of the night

11 *Tanacetum balsamita*, costmary

12 *Viola odorata*, sweet violet

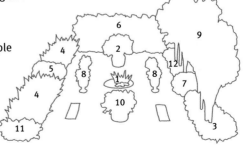

In addition to their cherished fruit, *Citrus* species and hybrids contribute fragrant foliage and flowers to the garden. If winters in your area are too cold for citrus, try growing one of the smaller varieties in a pot and move it indoors for the winter.

oils produced by special hairs on the leaves, known as trichomes. The hairs—often found on the leaves of herbs that evolved in warm, dry regions such as the Mediterranean, North Africa, and India—also help shade the rest of the leaf and combat transpiration and dehydration.

Fragrant flowers produce their perfumes in special glands on the petals known as osmophores. To do their job adequately, the osmophores must be exposed to the air and must receive certain nutrients from the roots, which explains why some fragrant blooms such as roses have little or no odor when they are cut in tight bud and left to open in a vase.

We register smells with the 5 million or so scent receptors in our noses (dogs boast an amazing 500 million of them). Still, what pleasure those mere 5 million scent receptors can afford.

Herbs for a Fragrant Garden

Acorus calamus
Calamus, Sweet Flag

Calamus is a vigorous, rhizomatous perennial that bears irislike fans of aromatic foliage up to four feet long. In the centuries before chemical air fresheners, the long, sword-shaped leaves of calamus were cut and placed on the floor. When people walked on them, they released their essential oils, freshening and perfuming the stale air. It is considered an aromatic bitter and at one time was used as a carminative to aid toothache, stomach ache, indigestion, as well as colds and coughs. Originally from temperate Asia and the southeastern United States, calamus is now widely naturalized throughout the Northern Hemisphere.

Growing Tips Moisture-loving calamus is tough and easily grown, and prefers full sun and damp or boggy soil. Plant it in areas that don't drain well and remain moist—where the roof gutters empty, in natural depressions, or at the bottom of

Acorus calamus, sweet flag.

a grade where water collects. Divide it every few years to keep it from taking over and to encourage fresh new leaves. Hardy in Zones 3 to 10.

Cultivars and Related Species *Acorus calamus* 'Variegata', which has cream-and-yellow-variegated foliage, is showier than the species and adds extra seasonal color to the landscape.

Companion Plants Create an aquatic herb garden by combining calamus with native white water-lilies (*Nymphaea alba* or *N. candida*), watercress (*Nasturtium officinale*), and arrowheads (*Sagittaria*).

Citrus species
Citrus

Citrus trees are highly decorative additions to the fragrant herb garden. They bear aromatic, glossy, dark green foliage, and the stems and branches of some species are heavily armed with sharp spines. Clusters of waxy, white, star-shaped blossoms with a heady perfume are borne in spring, followed by the botanical calling card of the genus, a modified berry called a hesperidium. In the ground, specimens may grow as tall as 30 feet. Potted trees are usually much smaller, up to 6 to 9 feet tall.

Growing Tips In frost-free climates, citrus trees flourish in fertile, well-drained soil in a sunny, protected spot. During active growth and flowering they need plenty of water and regular small applications of a nitrogenous fertilizer. Use greensand, compost, and composted manure. When grown indoors, potted trees require full sun and cool temperatures in winter and a vacation outdoors in summer whenever possible. Add coffee grounds or tea leaves to the potting mix to lower the pH as needed (5.5 to 6 is preferred). Watch for mealy bugs, scale, and spider mites. Hardy in Zones 9 to 12.

Cultivars and Related Species There are about 20 species of *Citrus* and innumerable hybrids and cultivars, including lime (*C.* × *aurantifolia*); sour orange (*C.* × *aurantium*); sweet orange (*C. sinensis*); grapefruit (*C.* × *paradisi*); pomelos, shaddocks, and uglis (*C. maxima* cultivars); lemon (*C.* × *limon*); citron (*C. medica*); mandarins, satsumas, and tangerines (*C. reticulata* cultivars); and calamondin orange (*C.* × *microcarpa*). A wonderful lemon cultivar, *C.* × *limon* 'Variegated Pink', bears variegated green-and-white foliage and green-and-yellow-striped fruit with pink flesh.

Companion Plants Use potted specimens throughout the garden, as a focal point in an herb bed or border, at the end of a garden path, or flanking an entranceway. For a heady collection in frost-free areas, combine *Citrus* with *Gardenia,* jasmine (*Jasminum*), and *Brugmansia.*

Convallaria majalis
Lily-of-the-Valley

The intensely sweet-smelling lily-of-the-valley is one of the true harbingers of spring and reigns supreme as the official flower of May. This old-fashioned favorite has escaped countless old herb and flower gardens across the United States and Canada to colonize areas surrounding farmhouses, hedgerows, and second-growth forests in the East and South. This herbaceous perennial produces four- to eight-inch lance-shaped foliage and delicate spikes of bell-shaped white flowers in May or early June. Plants grow vigorously, forming clumps that can cover 20 to 40 inches in diameter.

Growing Tips Lilies-of-the-valley prefer dappled shade and deep, moist, fertile, well-drained soil. Surround their allotted space with sunken plastic edging to a depth of 12 inches to keep them within limits. Propagate by division of the creeping, thickened roots, known as pips. You can dig clusters of pips in autumn after the plants have gone dormant and pot them for wintertime forcing. Hardy in Zones 3 to 9.

Cultivars and Related Species *Convallaria majalis* 'Albostriata' has dark leaves with white to cream stripes; 'Aureovariegata' (syn. 'Striata') has gold-striped leaves; 'Aureomarginata' has cream- to yellow-edged foliage; and 'Hardwick Hall' produces very broad leaves with pale margins. 'Prolificans' displays unusually and variably shaped starry white blossoms. *Convallaria majalis* var. *rosea* bears small pale pink flowers.

Companion Plants For a unique effect, combine all the excellent cultivars of lily-of-the-valley along a border. Alternately, team it with variegated money plant (*Lunaria annua* 'Variegata').

Iris pallida
Iris germanica var. florentina
Orris Root

Both *Iris pallida* and *I. germanica* var. *florentina* have fragrant rhizomes (botanically speaking, these are fleshy horizontal stems, not roots) used in perfume. Typical German bearded-type irises, they bear white to palest violet to light blue flowers on two- to three-foot-tall scapes in June, which are so deliciously fragrant that they alone make these plants worth growing. The rhizomes contain irone, the compound that gives sweet violets (*Viola odorata*, page 98) their distinct fragrance. Freshly peeled rhizomes of orris root are typically earthy smelling but develop the classic violetlike perfume,

Iris germanica var. florentina, orris root.

foliage marked white on the leaf margins, provide color throughout the growing season when the plants are not in flower.

Companion Plants For a stellar mélange, combine orris root with yellow-flowered *Iris pseudacorus* 'Variegata', which bears tall, yellow-variegated foliage. Or dot variegated cultivars in clumps throughout the herb bed for continual foliage color. When using iris in a mixed border, leave plenty of room around it to deter rhizome rot and iris borer.

Melissa officinalis 'Aurea'
Variegated Lemon Balm

The scent of lemons is one of the most popular and memorable of garden fragrances. Variegated *Melissa officinalis* 'Aurea' bears green, slightly fuzzy foliage with fantastic gold splotches; when crushed, the leaves release a lemony fragrance. 'Aurea' is infinitely more ornamental than the species itself. Plants can grow 24 to 36 inches tall and 18 inches wide. Insignificant white blossoms appear during summer.

which evolves best over two or more years as the rhizomes dry. Fresh rhizomes are high in vitamin C and make a perfumed tea to assist in fighting the common cold. Candied rhizomes, once an important Victorian sweetmeat, provide a strong, but pleasant-tasting expectorant and breath freshener.

Growing Tips Like other bearded irises, they prefer full sun and average, well-drained soil. Divide clumps every three to four years and save the rhizomes' terminal growths, consisting of two or three fans. In areas where iris borer is prevalent, allow the newly divided fans to sun-cure for a few days before replanting. Throw away grub-riddled rhizomes—don't compost them. Hardy in Zones 5 to 9.

Cultivars and Related Species *Iris pallida* 'Variegata', with creamy-yellow stripes, and *I. pallida* 'Argentea Variegata', with

Melissa officinalis 'Aurea', variegated lemon balm.

Passiflora incarnata, maypop.

Growing Tips and Cultivars and Related Species See *Melissa officinalis*, page 44. Seedlings of 'Aurea' are usually plain green, so propagate this cultivar by stem or root cuttings or by division.

Companion Plants Blend Melissa *officinalis* 'Aurea' with other bright-leafed herbs such as white-variegated peppermint (*Mentha* × *piperata* 'Variegata'); variegated red mint (M. × gracilis 'Variegata'), with comely yellow-streaked foliage; and variegated sage (*Salvia officinalis* 'Tricolor'), with dull green leaves edged with yellow and salmon pink.

Passiflora incarnata
Maypop

The three-inch-long lavender-and-white tubular flowers of this highly ornamental flowering and fruiting vine are wildly attractive to hummingbirds, bees, and butterflies. The fruit, a fragrant yellow, hard-skinned two- to three-inch berry, has perfumed, gelatinous flesh studded with crunchy, flavorful seeds. Medium green foliage is six inches long and three-lobed. The plant climbs vigorously with the aid of long, strong tendrils. In Florida, it is an important larval food plant for visiting tropical butterflies such as heliconians.

Growing Tips Maypop prefers full sun but will tolerate partial shade in fertile, well-drained soil enhanced with compost or rotted manure. Cultivate it on a sturdy trellis, pergola, gazebo, or archway, or train it on a wall, supported by guylines. A succession of arches covered with maypop scrambling to form a roof over a path or walkway is particularly effective. Maypop can be evergreen in southern areas; in northern zones, dig the thickened roots up in fall and overwinter them as you would dahlias. For earlier bloom, start them on a sunny windowsill before planting out. Propagate through cuttings or ground layering (pegging). Hardy in Zones 5 to 9.

Cultivars and Related Species *Passiflora incarnata* 'Alba' bears pure white blossoms. A Brazilian species, *P. edulis,* called parcha or granadilla, bears white flowers with white and purple-banded filaments and produces delectably succulent fruit. This species is only hardy to Zones 10 to 12; overwinter it in a greenhouse in the north.

Companion Plants This glorious vine is best appreciated alone but can be combined with low-growing, well-behaved herbs such as sage (*Salvia* species and cultivars, pages 36, 47, 48, 58, 111), marjoram (*Origanum majorana*, page 56), and hyssop (*Hyssopus officinalis*), leaving an 18-inch plant-free zone around its base to avoid root competition.

Podophyllum peltatum
May Apple

This stoutly rhizomatous woodland native produces a single pair of three- to nine-lobed, foot-wide leaves. A single nodding, parasol-shaped, fragrant white to pink-blushed blossom is produced in the leaf joint. The plant can reach a height and spread of 24 inches. A three-inch, egg-shaped fruit ripens July through early September as the foliage withers toward dormancy. The unripe fruit is toxic, but it's edible when mature: Eat the yellowish, soft, and highly fragrant fruit fresh out of hand or make it into jams, jellies, or pastry creams. A fresh fruit tart made with May apples will drive your guests to distraction.

Podophyllum peltatum, **May apple.**

Growing Tips May apple prefers rich, moisture-retentive soil in high dappled shade. It is most often propagated from division or seed. May apple is extremely attractive to squirrels, chipmunks, and field mice; try deflecting them with anti-bird netting designed for blueberries and strawberries. Hardy in Zones 4 to 6.

Cultivars and Related Species The Himalayan May apple, *Podophyllum hexandrum,* grows about 16 inches tall and wide and produces delicious, very bright orange-red fruit.

Companion Plants Combine May apple with other North American wildflowers such as wake robins (*Trillium*), foamflowers (*Tiarella*), wild ginger (*Asarum canadense,* page 78), and columbines (*Aquilegia*).

Pogostemon cablin • Patchouli

Patchouli has one of the most permeating and heady scents of any herb, which

makes it truly a love-it-or-leave-it plant. It is rarely cultivated in North America—a shame indeed, because it is eminently gardenworthy. This attractive, soft-leafed tender perennial, often grown as an annual, has square stems and opposite foliage with serrated margins that look surprisingly like maple leaves. The plant can grow to three feet tall and spread about two feet wide. Small-lipped, tubular white flowers tinged with purple appear in September and October.

Growing Tips Patchouli relishes the heat and high humidity of summer and is perfectly suited to southern gardens. Give it full sun or partial shade and very rich, moisture-retentive soil amended with compost or well-rotted manure. Northern gardeners can try it as an annual herb outdoors or experiment with windowsill culture indoors (watch for mealy bug and whitefly). If grown inside give it full sun and keep the soil

evenly moist but not soggy. Hardy in Zones 10 to 11.

Cultivars and Related Species None.

Companion Plants To play up patchouli's natural insecticidal qualities, use it as an edging plant for beds of sweet-scented roses, lilies, cheddar pinks (*Dianthus gratianopolitanus*, page 107), or irises (*Iris pallida*, page 92). Or surround your vegetable or fruit garden with it.

Sassafras albidum
Sassafras

Sassafras trees are native to the forests of the northeastern United States and are known for their aromatic foliage, bark, and roots. The essential oils from the roots and inner stem bark contain the compound safrole, which native Americans relied on to help heal insect bites, poison ivy, kidney ailments, hypertension, and other ailments. The dried, pulverized foliage is the ubiquitous filet gumbo of Cajun and Creole cooking—used to thicken soups and stews. Sassafras foliage is dark green and slightly pubescent, ranging in shape from simple ovate to bilobed (really mitten-shaped) to trilobed—and all forms may be borne on the same twig. The leaves turn vivid gold and red in fall.

Growing Tips Sassafras develops into a fairly substantial tree about 50 feet tall and 30 feet wide, but it can be maintained at a much smaller, manageable size by judicious pruning. It prefers deep, water-retentive (but not soggy) soil amended with plenty of leaf mold, compost, or composted manure. Grow it in full sun or partial shade. Propagation is very easy using suckers, small divisions, or root cuttings. Hardy in Zones 5 to 9.

Pogostemon cablin, patchouli.

Sassafras albidum, sassafras.

Cultivars and Related Species None.

Companion Plants Grow sassafras as a small tree to create shade in a garden of shade-loving herbs such as Solomon's seal (*Polygonatum biflorum*), May apple (*Podophyllum peltatum*, page 95), lily-of-the-valley (*Convallaria majalis*, page 92), sweet woodruff (*Galium odoratum*, page 80), and *Rodgersia*. Or combine it with witch-hazel (*Hamamelis*), Florida allspice (*Calycanthus floridus*), bayberry (*Morella pensylvanica* syn. *Myrica pensylvanica*), and summersweet (*Clethra alnifolia*).

Selenicereus grandiflorus
Queen of the Night, Night-Blooming Cereus

Cacti are not usually found on lists of fragrant herbs, but this one has a rightful place here. It plays an important role in the herbal lore of its native Mexico, Puerto Rico, and the eastern Caribbean. The juice of the stems and flowers is used to prepare a tonic to strengthen the muscles of the heart—it possesses properties similar to those of digitalis. From July through September, this species produces some of the most spectacular and strongly perfumed flowers of any cactus. The huge blossoms, up to 16 inches long and 10 inches wide, open after midnight—to be pollinated by nectar-feeding bats in the cactus's native habitat in Mexico and the West Indies—only to whither by morning. The plant itself is no great beauty, however. The shallow-ribbed stems bear bristly clusters of sharp spines as well as aerial roots. Plants grow in a "sausage-link style" and grapple upward to 17 feet. They need a sturdy support system or hanging basket to keep them in bounds.

Growing Tips Queen of the night requires full sun and fertile, compost- or manure-enhanced but impeccably drained soil. If necessary, add coarse sand or turkey grit and horticultural charcoal to aid drainage. Propagation is easy from stem cuttings. In colder climates, cultivate it in a greenhouse or sunroom, with a summer vacation outdoors, if possible. Watch out for scale and mealy bugs. Hardy in Zones 9 to 12.

Cultivars and Related Species As yet there are no cultivars. A related genus, *Hylacereus*, bears intensely fragrant flowers 8 to 12 inches long and wide; *H. undatus,* also known as night-blooming cereus, scrambles as high as 20 feet. Cultivate these like *Selenicereus grandiflorus.*

Companion Plants Use this cactus alone to better admire its severe architectural form. Or, in areas where it can be culti-vated outdoors, combine it with prickly pear cactus (*Opuntia ficus-indica*), aloes (*Aloe vera; A. barbadense*), and mother-of-thousands (*Kalanchoe pinnatum*), to create an herbal cactus and succulent garden.

Tanacetum balsamita
Costmary

Costmary is a wonderful perennial herb cherished for its minty-smelling foliage with hints of balsam, as its species name, *balsamita*, implies. It bears smooth, fairly dark green, 5- to 12-inch-long and 2-inch-wide foliage with delicately serrated margins. It can reach 3 feet tall and 18 inches wide under ideal conditions. Small, somewhat insignificant button-shaped yellow flowers arrive in mid- to late summer. Rub the bruised leaves on insect bites and stings to relieve pain.

Growing Tips Costmary prefers full sun but will tolerate partial shade. Average garden soil and moisture are adequate. Propagate costmary by stem or root cuttings or by division. Remove its flower spikes to encourage the production of fresh foliage. Hardy in Zones 4 to 8.

Cultivars and Related Species None.

Companion Plants Costmary combines nicely with other herbs from the aster family: 'Powis Castle' wormwood (*Artemisia* 'Powis Castle'), coneflowers (*Echinacea*), calendulas, stevia (*Stevia rebaudiana,* page TH), and goldenrods (*Solidago*). It's also effective in rock gardens, wall plantings, and trough gardens.

Viola odorata
Sweet Violet

The edible flowers of early-spring-blooming sweet violet are very fragrant

Tanacetum balsamita, costmary.

Viola odorata, **sweet violet.**

and range from pure white to pale lavender (or bicolor) to deep blue and, very rarely, yellow. This perennial grows four to six inches tall and can spread up to two feet by profusely produced short runners. The dark green foliage is heart-shaped and two to three inches long and wide.

Growing Tips Sweet violets excel in full sun or dappled shade in a humus- or compost-rich soil that holds moisture but doesn't remain soggy. Propagate them by division. Sweet violets are prolific seeders (to the point of weediness), but volunteers typically revert to the deep blue form. Hardy in Zones 6 to 10.

Cultivars and Related Species *Viola odorata* 'Purple Robe' has masses of deep purple flowers. 'Admiral Avellan' produces fragrant, purplish-red flowers; 'Coeur d'Alsace' bears salmon-pink blossoms. 'Alba' produces single, pure white flowers, and 'Alba Plena de Cheuvereuse' shows double white. The very fragrant 'Countess of Shaftesbury' bears medium blue, pink-centered flowers; 'John Raddenbury' is medium blue with white eyes. The choice variety 'Mrs. R. Barton' bears white-dotted, mauve blossoms.

Companion Plants Try sweet violets as edging plants, in trough gardens or rock gardens, and in wall plantings or high raised beds where it's easier to enjoy their perfume. Or team them with variegated lungwort (*Pulmonaria* 'Silver Streamers') and brunnera (*Brunnera macrophylla* 'Davison's White'), with cream-and-green leaves and light blue blossoms.

Designing an Herb Garden for Butterflies

Claire Hagen Dole

Many of my favorite images from the garden have to do with butterflies and herbs: a tawny skipper on dark purple oregano, caught by late-afternoon sun; or the large, yellow wings of a tiger swallowtail fluttering over fragrant lavender. I've watched a fat caterpillar, boldly striped in yellow, green, and black, munching on delicate fennel leaves, then, a few weeks later, emerging as a beautiful yellow and black anise swallowtail from its chrysalis on the fennel stalk to take flight.

Complementing the busy hum of honeybees and bumblebees, butterflies bring color and motion to the herb garden. Flitting from thyme to lavender, taking nectar from catmint, or basking on sun-warmed stones, they are lovely to behold and fascinating to observe up close.

In spring, whites, admirals, hairstreaks, and blues are attracted to early-blooming chives, calendula, and dandelions. Summer brings a bounty of fritillaries, admirals, sulphurs, painted ladies, and many other butterflies into the garden. Butterfly magnets include several North American native herbs in addition to traditional herb garden plants: mountain mint (*Pycnanthemum muticum*), milkweeds (*Asclepias*), anise hyssop (*Agastache foeniculum*), and bee balms (*Monarda*). Bee balms, which are attractive to hummingbirds and butterflies, come in many appealing forms—from the tiered pink

Continued on page 104

The same thing that attracts people to a garden attracts butterflies too—flowers, and lots of them, providing nectar-laden blooms from spring to fall. In mid- to late summer, the flowers of sweet joe-pye weed, *Eupatorium purpureum*, opposite, draw many butterflies, such as this monarch.

An Herb Garden for Butterflies

Many herbs that are popular with people are also butterfly favorites since they are close to their wild form and thus rich in nectar. Marjoram (*Origanum majorana*) and spike lavender (*Lavandula latifolia*) are good examples. The insects often become so engrossed in sipping nectar from the flowers that you can approach them slowly to observe them with a hand lens. Butterflies aren't fussy about garden style; just about any design will do. Just be sure to locate the garden in a sunny spot, sheltered from the wind, where butterflies can bask and warm themselves. They are ectothermic and need to warm their bodies before taking flight. Steppingstones and rock walls, both common elements of herb gardens, are perfect for this purpose. And keep in mind that drifts of the individual herbs in your garden are more likely to entice passing butterflies—and keep them lingering—than lone specimens. For favorite butterfly flowers, see pages 106 to 112.

Design Tips

- To boost your garden's appeal to a wide variety of butterflies, plant clumps of herbs with different flower colors, sizes, and shapes.

- Provide plants not just for butterflies but also for their offspring. For a list of caterpillar favorites, see page 105.

- Transform that traditional herb garden element, the boxwood (*Buxus*) hedge, into a butterfly attraction by using rosemary (*Rosmarinus officinalis*), santolinas, lavenders (*Lavandula*), or germander (*Teucrium chamaedrys*) instead.

- Some butterflies engage in a behavior called puddling—sipping minerals from wet sand or soil. Provide a safe spot for them to puddle by mounding some wet sand in an unused birdbath, out of reach of pouncing cats.

Plants Featured in This Garden

1 *Achillea millefolium* 'Cerise Queen', 'Cerise Queen' yarrow

2 *Allium cernuum*, nodding onion

3 *Asclepias speciosa*, showy milkweed

4 *Dianthus gratianopolitanus*, cheddar pink

5 *Eupatorium purpureum*, sweet joe-pye weed

6 *Foeniculum vulgare* 'Purpurascens', bronze fennel

7 *Lavandula latifolia*, spike lavender

8 *Origanum laevigatum* 'Herrenhausen', 'Herrenhausen' oregano

9 *Salvia* 'Indigo Spires', 'Indigo Spires' sage

10 *Tagetes tenuifolia* 'Lemon Gem', 'Lemon Gem' signet marigold

11 *Thymus vulgaris* 'Narrow Leaf French', French thyme

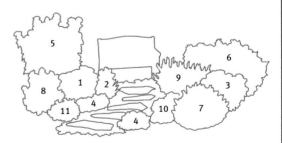

blooms of lemon mint (*M. citriodora*) to Oswego tea (*M. didyma*), a red flower that has been bred into many cultivars, such as 'Cambridge Scarlet' (page 45).

In autumn, it's especially important to provide nectar plants for migrating monarchs and other late-season butterflies, such as skippers and red admirals. Make room in your herb garden for late bloomers like signet marigold (*Tagetes tenuifolia*), joe-pye weed *(Eupatorium),* pineapple sage (*Salvia elegans*), and goldenrods (*Solidago*). Monarchs, which can travel up to 80 miles a day during migration, are highly attracted to seaside goldenrod (*Solidago sempervirens*), an enthusiasm they share with scores of other beneficial insects. And when the butterflies are finished with the spent blooms of goldenrod or spike lavender, watch finches and sparrows make a meal off their seeds.

Hosting Caterpillars

A butterfly goes through four distinct stages during its life cycle: egg, larva (caterpillar), pupa (chrysalis), and adult. The larva is an eating machine, bulking up a thousandfold on a diet of leaves and buds. To accomplish this phenomenal growth, it sheds its too-tight exoskeleton several times, swallowing air to expand and then harden its new skin.

Egg-laying female butterflies carefully choose the plants that their larvae will feed on. They scratch leaf surfaces with special receptors on their feet, giving the leaves a chemical "taste test" to ensure that they are appropriate. Some butterflies are very particular: Monarchs lay eggs only on milkweeds; fritillaries choose violets (*Viola*). Others, such as the painted lady, accept up to a hundred different caterpillar host plants.

If you grow parsley (*Petroselinum crispum* var. *neapolitanum* or *P. crispum* var. *crispum*), dill (*Anethum graveolens*), caraway (*Carum carvi*), or fennel (*Foeniculum vulgare*) in your herb garden, you're likely to discover the colorful larvae of black or anise swallowtails on the foliage. Just plant a little extra to share with the black, green, and yellow caterpillars.

You may also find them feeding on foliage of lovage (*Levisticum officinale*) and angelica (*Angelica archangelica*). Plant nasturtiums (*Tropaeolum*) to lure the cabbage

Adults in search of nectar aren't the only butterflies happy to visit the herb garden. Female butterflies find many plants suitable for laying eggs, providing human visitors with ample opportunities for watching caterpillars like this black swallowtail.

Herbs That Feed Caterpillars

Achillea millefolium 'Cerise Queen', 'Cerise Queen' yarrow, page 106	Painted lady
Anethum graveolens, dill, page 29	Black and anise swallowtails
Angelica archangelica, angelica, page 77	Black and anise swallowtails
Asclepias speciosa, showy milkweed, page 107	Monarch, queen
Foeniculum vulgare, fennel, page 67, 109	Black and anise swallowtails
Melissa officinalis, lemon balm, page 44	White peacock
Mentha species and cultivars, mints, pages 31, 44	White peacock, painted lady
Passiflora incarnata, maypop, page 94	Gulf fritillary
Petroselinum crispum, parsley, page 34	Black and anise swallowtails
Rumex sanguineus, bloody sorrel, page 20	Coppers, painted lady
Ruta graveolens, rue, page 21	Black and giant swallowtails
Salvia species, sages, pages 36, 47, 48, 58, 111	Painted lady, gray hairstreak
Sassafras albidum, sassafras, page 96	Spicebush swallowtail
Tanacetum balsamita, costmary, page 98	Painted lady
Viola odorata, sweet violet, page 98	Fritillaries

white away from your arugula; its leaves contain oils that are chemically similar.

Some herb gardeners grow nettles (*Urtica dioica*) for use as a spring tonic or as a dye component. Allow nettles to grow at the garden's edge, and you may be rewarded with larvae of the red admiral, painted lady, satyr comma, or Milbert's tortoiseshell. All of these larvae grow to $1\frac{1}{2}$ inches in length and are covered with branched spines— wicked barbs designed to repel predators. Painted lady caterpillars may also be seen on the foliage of yarrows (*Achillea*), wormwoods (*Artemisia*), borage (*Borago officinalis*), curry plant (*Helichrysum angustifolium*), mints (*Mentha*), sages (*Salvia*), comfrey (*Symphytum*), and tansy (*Tanacetum*).

In most cases, caterpillars will not completely defoliate a plant. If you're worried about their impact, it's easy to relocate a few larvae to another, similar plant. Put on a pair of garden gloves—in case the larvae are spiny—and gently pick off the caterpillar and place it on another plant, making sure it has a grip on it before you let go. You can carry it in the palm of your hand, but don't squeeze it. Besides growing into lovely herb-pollinating butterflies, larvae are an important source of protein in the food web, forming part of a diverse ecosystem of birds, lizards, small mammals, wasps, and spiders in the herb garden.

Allium cernuum, **nodding onion.**

Herbs to Attract Butterflies

Achillea millefolium 'Cerise Queen'
'Cerise Queen' Yarrow

'Cerise Queen' offers abundant blooms in shades of magenta from June until September. Flower stalks, with lacy green foliage, reach up to three feet high. Flat, sturdy umbels provide a good landing pad for many butterflies, including skippers, hairstreaks, and painted ladies.

Growing Tips Easy to start from seed, yarrow does well in full sun and lean soil. It is drought-tolerant and may become quite aggressive. Deadhead it to encourage new bloom. 'Cerise Queen' has good color retention when dried. Hardy in Zones 3 to 10.

Cultivars and Related Species *Achillea* 'Paprika' forms large clusters of bright red flowers, which fade to pink as they age. It has deep green, fernlike foliage and reaches two feet high; it requires richer soil and more regular watering.

Drought-tolerant *Achillea filipendulina* 'Moonshine' is a few inches shorter, with yellow blooms and silvery foliage. Both plants bloom all summer long.

Companion Plants Team yarrow with 'Lemon Gem' signet marigold (*Tagetes tenuifolia* 'Lemon Gem', page 111) and oregano 'Herrenhausen' (*Origanum laevigatum* 'Herrenhausen', page 110). Or try combining it with the yellow blooms of *Coreopsis verticillata* 'Moonbeam'; the tall, white spikes of Culver's root (*Veronicastrum virginicum*); and feathery stalks of fountain grass (*Pennisetum alopecuroides* 'Hameln').

Allium cernuum • Nodding Onion

This North American native forms dense clumps of grasslike leaves and drooping clusters of white flowers on stalks up to two feet high. Flowers open in midsummer and turn pink as they age. The nectar is attractive to small butterflies like blues, hairstreaks, and whites.

Growing Tips Nodding onion is easy to grow from seed and likes average to rich, well-drained soil in full sun. Divide clumps in fall or early spring. Hardy in Zones 4 to 8.

Cultivars and Related Species Autumn onion (*Allium stellatum*), another North American native, resembles nodding onion but holds its umbel of flowers erect. Its leaves are narrow; flower stalks reach one foot high. Garden chives (*Allium schoenoprasum*) have pink flowers and pungent, tubular leaves; the plants reach one foot high.

Companion Plants Plant nodding onion in drifts next to the tall, pink flowers of mallows (*Malva; Sidalcea*) or purple coneflower (*Echinacea purpurea*). They are also lovely next to sage (*Salvia officinalis* hybrids and cultivars, pages 36, 47, 48, 58, 111) and lavenders (*Lavandula* hybrids and cultivars, pages 55, 68, 109).

Asclepias speciosa
Showy Milkweed

This lovely North American native bears clusters of star-shaped pink flowers on three-foot stalks, with wide, velvety leaves in a soft shade of gray-green. Showy milkweed blooms in early summer, attracting a wide variety of butterflies. Monarch caterpillars feed on its leaves, ingesting toxins that make them unpalatable to predators.

Growing Tips Once established, showy milkweed is drought-tolerant. Grow it in full sun, in average soil. The plant spreads by rhizomes to form a clump. The attractive seedpods release downy seeds in late fall. Gather and keep the pods indoors until spring, then set them

Asclepias speciosa, showy milkweed.

outside for hummingbirds to glean as nesting material. Hardy in Zones 4 to 9.

Cultivars and Related Species Drought-tolerant butterfly weed (*Asclepias tuberosa*) has narrower leaves, clusters of bright orange blossoms, and reaches three feet high. It forms a deep taproot, which does not do well in wet soil. *Asclepias tuberosa* 'Hello Yellow' and 'Gay Butterflies' are seed mixes of red, yellow, and orange flowers.

Companion Plants Combine showy milkweed with wild bergamot (*Monarda fistulosa*, page 83), meadow, or Rocky Mountain, blazingstar (*Liatris ligulistylus*), and purple coneflower (*Echinacea purpurea*).

Dianthus gratianopolitanus
Cheddar pink

This heirloom herb, known for its spicy fragrance, is attractive to many butterflies and night-flying moths. Its bright

Dianthus gratianopolitanus, **cheddar pinks.**

pink blossoms, which form on ten-inch stalks from midsummer to early fall, have a darker center, and petals have a ragged fringe. The narrow, grayish-green leaves form a clump that's attractive even when the plant's not in bloom.

Growing Tips Pinks like full sun and good drainage; they need supplemental watering in summer. They are easy to grow from seed or propagate by cutting or layering. Replace this short-lived perennial every three years. Hardy in Zones 3 to 10.

Cultivars and Related Species *Dianthus gratianopolitanus* 'Tiny Rubies' is charming next to paving stones or in a rock garden. It forms a four-inch-high mat of blue-green leaves covered with fragrant pink flowers in late spring. Sweet William (*D. barbatus*), a short-lived perennial or biennial reaching one to two feet high, is noted for its heady scent. Its flowers may be white, pink, or red, often with contrasting bands of color along the edges or in the center.

Companion Plants Plant cheddar pinks next to lavender (*Lavandula* species, hybrids, and cultivars, pages 55, 68, 109), catmint (*Nepeta cataria*), or the silvery foliage of Russian tarragon (*Artemisia dracunculus*) or 'Powis Castle' wormwood (*Artemisia* 'Powis Castle').

Eupatorium purpureum
Sweet Joe-Pye Weed

The large clusters of fuzzy, dusty rose blooms of this perennial herb are magnets for swallowtails, monarchs, and other butterflies from midsummer to early fall, and its seed heads are attractive in winter. Joe-pye weed's six-foot stalks, adorned with large, crinkly leaves, grow from thick clumps.

Growing Tips Native to moist meadows of eastern North America, joe-pye weed tolerates many soil types but may require supplemental watering in summer. Plant it in full sun or light shade. Thin the clumps to improve air circulation if powdery mildew is a problem, and divide clumps in spring or fall. Hardy in Zones 4 to 9.

Cultivars and Related Species Mistflower (*Eupatorium coelestinum*) grows two to three feet high, with very fuzzy clusters of lavender-blue flowers. It spreads rapidly by rhizomes and tolerates dry soil. Blooming from late summer to frost, mistflower is highly attractive to late-season butterflies such as monarchs, skippers, and sulphurs. Spotted joe-pye weed (*E. maculatum*), another butterfly favorite, reaches five to seven feet, with huge clusters of dusty rose blooms in late summer. It thrives in rich, moist soil and full sun but needs plenty of space.

Companion Plants Joe-pye weed looks wonderful with its meadow companions bee balms (*Monarda; M. didyma* 'Cambridge Scarlet', page 45), purple coneflower (*Echinacea purpurea*), sneezeweed (*Helenium autumnale*), goldenrods (*Solidago*), and blazingstars (*Liatris*).

Foeniculum vulgare 'Purpurascens'
'Purpurascens' Bronze Fennel

This highly decorative form of fennel grows to five feet with lacy bronze-red foliage. Its color is strongest in spring. Small butterflies and beneficial insects are drawn to the umbels of yellow flowers in summer. Caterpillars of black swallowtail and anise swallowtail, decoratively striped in yellow, green, and black, feed on its leaves.

Foeniculum vulgare 'Purpurascens', bronze fennel.

Growing Tips See *Foeniculum vulgare* 'Rubrum', page 67. Don't plant bronze fennel near dill (*Anethum graveolens*, page 29), as the two plants will cross-pollinate. Swallowtail chrysalides may overwinter on the stalks, so leave them through the winter or check before cutting them back in late fall.

Cultivars and Related Species Common fennel (*F. vulgare*) has green foliage and umbels of yellow flowers in summer and reaches four feet in height.

Companion Plants Fennel is useful in the vegetable garden because it attracts parasitic wasps, ladybird beetles, and tachinid flies, which prey on insect pests. Plant it next to basils (*Ocimum basilicum* cultivars, pages 18, 32, 68), nasturtiums (*Tropaeolum*), and petunias (*Petunia*).

Lavandula latifolia
Spike Lavender

Spike lavender has violet-green flower heads on long stalks, with grayish-green,

broad leaves that give off a resinous fragrance. Not as colorful as English lavender (*Lavandula angustifolia*), with which it is crossed to create lavandins (*L. × intermedia*), spike lavender grows to two feet tall and blooms from late August to mid-October. It's very attractive to skippers, buckeyes, painted ladies, and bumblebees. In late fall, juncos feed on its seeds.

Growing Tips See *Lavandula angustifolia* 'Royal Velvet', page 55. Propagate spike lavender by cuttings or seeds. Shear it back in late fall after birds have gleaned its seeds. Hardy in Zones 7 to 9.

Cultivars and Related Species Lavandins (*L. × intermedia*) are taller, with long stems that make great wands. 'Hidcote Giant' has large, violet flower heads on 2½-foot stalks. 'Provence', with violet flowers on 2½-foot stalks, makes a good hedge plant. See also 'Grosso', page 55.

Companion Plants For season-long attraction of butterflies, combine late-blooming spike lavender with other lavenders (*Lavendula,* pages 55, 68, 109), oreganos (*Origanum × majoricum*, page 33, *O. laevigatum* 'Herrenhausen', page 110), and blue fescue (*Festuca glauca*).

Origanum laevigatum 'Herrenhausen' 'Herrenhausen' Oregano

'Herrenhausen' is a hardy ornamental oregano covered with clusters of deep purple bracts topped with tiny pink flowers from midsummer to early fall, attracting skippers, whites, and hairstreaks. The dark green leaves of this two-foot-tall plant have a fruity scent. The flowers are beautiful in dried arrangements.

Growing Tips *Origanum* 'Herrenhausen' is a vigorous grower in full sun and well-drained, average soil. Propagate it by cuttings or division. It will self-seed readily; shear it after blooming in fall. Hardy in Zones 5 to 9.

Cultivars and Related Species *Origanum laevigatum* 'Hopley's' is similar to 'Herrenhausen' but more compact (to 18 inches). Its deep purple flowers bloom all summer, attracting many bees and butterflies. Compact oregano (*O. vulgare* 'Compactum'), which has a creeping growth habit, makes a nice groundcover or rock garden plant, reaching eight inches high. It has greenish-purple flower heads and strongly scented, dark green leaves. Grow it in full sun. See also *Origanum vulgare* subsp. *hirtum* 'Kalitera', page 56, and marjoram (*O. majorana*), page 56.

Companion Plants Grow 'Herrenhausen' next to pink-flowering caraway thyme (*Thymus herba-barona*, page 23) and

Origanum laevigatum 'Herrenhausen', 'Herrenhausen' oregano.

Mexican bush sage (*Salvia leucantha*), which has fuzzy purple blooms.

Salvia 'Indigo Spires'
'Indigo Spires' Sage

Large and showy, 'Indigo Spires' has long, twisting stems covered with blue-purple flowers and fragrant dark green, scalloped leaves. It has a bushlike habit, growing to four feet or higher, and blooms from early summer until frost. It attracts swallowtails, buckeyes, and west coast ladies.

Growing Tips See *Salvia officinalis* 'Woodcote Farm', page 48. Propagate 'Indigo Spires' by cuttings in spring or fall. Hardy in Zones 7 to 10.

Cultivars and Related Species Pineapple sage (*Salvia elegans*, page 47) is named for its pineapple-scented leaves. If you have moist soil, plant bog sage (*Salvia uliginosa*): Its five-foot stems, topped with clusters of sky-blue flowers, sway gracefully in the breeze and attract monarchs and bumblebees. Bog sage spreads quickly by underground rhizomes.

Companion Plants The deep blue-purple blooms of *Salvia* 'Indigo Spires' look stunning next to yellow flowers such as moonshine yarrow (*Achillea filipendulina* 'Moonshine'), 'Lemon Gem' signet marigold (*Tagetes tenuifolia* 'Lemon Gem', page 111), or milkweed (*Asclepias tuberosa* 'Hello Yellow').

Tagetes tenuifolia 'Lemon Gem'
'Lemon Gem' Signet Marigold

An annual from Mexico, signet marigold has lacy, citrus-scented foliage covered with many small, single-petaled flowers in shades of lemon, tangerine, or paprika. The flowers are edible and look pretty in salads. 'Lemon Gem' has five bright yel-

Salvia 'Indigo Spires', sage 'Indigo Spires'.

low petals around orange tube flowers and is highly attractive to small butterflies such as hairstreaks, whites, and blues. It blooms from midsummer to frost; the plants grow to one foot in height.

Growing Tips Marigolds are easy to grow in average soil and full sun to partial shade. Plant seeds outdoors in late spring or start seedlings indoors. Overwatering causes the plants to be leggy, with fewer blooms. Deadhead signet marigolds to prolong the bloom of this true annual. Plant 'Lemon Gem' in containers or as a hedge along a walkway.

Cultivars and Related Species French marigold (*T. patula*), with its single or double petals, is an easy-to-grow old-fashioned annual that draws butterflies into the garden. Among the many selections of this one- to two-foot-tall marigold is the striped 'Mr. Majestic',

Tagetes tenuifolia 'Lemon Gem', 'Lemon Gem' signet marigold.

which blooms in shades of gold, dark orange, and brick red.

Companion Plants Plant signet marigolds with red-flowering sages like *Salvia elegans* (page 47) or *S. greggi*, or with blue-blossomed spike speedwell (*Veronica spicata*).

Thymus vulgaris 'Narrow Leaf French' French Thyme

French thyme is a tidy, upright shrub with narrow gray-green leaves and pale lavender flowers. More strongly scented than English thyme, it is a good culinary variety. These plants reach ten inches in height and work well in containers or as edging. The flowers bloom in summer and are attractive to hairstreaks, skippers, and honeybees.

Growing Tips Grow French thyme in well-drained, sandy soil and full sun. Cut the woody stems back in spring to encourage new growth. Propagate it by division or root cuttings. French thyme may need some protection in cold-winter areas. Hardy in Zones 4 to 9.

Cultivars and Related Species Crimson thyme (*Thymus praecox* subsp. *brittanicus* 'Coccineus') is a creeping thyme with dark green leaves and tiny, deep rose flowers that bloom in summer. It looks wonderful interplanted with woolly thyme (*T. lanuginosus*) between stepping stones. Woolly thyme has soft, gray-green leaves; it may produce a few pale-pink flowers but is grown mainly for its texture. Both creeping thymes can easily be propagated by stem cuttings. They prefer well-drained, sandy soil.

Companion Plants Low-growing French thyme sets off taller herbs such as English lavender (*Lavandula angustifolia; L. angustifolia* 'Royal Velvet', page 55) and yarrow (*Achillea; A. millefolium* 'Cerise Queen', page 106). It contrasts beautifully with the deep pink blooms and grasslike foliage of cottage pink (*Dianthus plumarius*) or sea thrift (*Armeria maritima*).

USDA Hardiness Zone Map

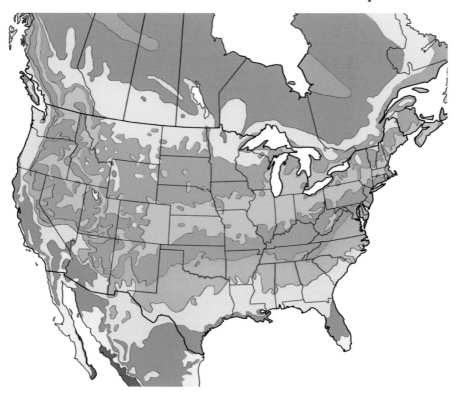

Zones and Minimum Winter Temperatures (°F.)

Zone 1 below −50°

Zone 2 −50° to −40°

Zone 3 −40° to −30°

Zone 4 −30° to −20°

Zone 5 −20° to 10°

Zone 6 −10° to 0°

Zone 7 0° to 10°

Zone 8 10° to 20°

Zone 9 20° to 30°

Zone 10 30° to 40°

Zone 11 above 40°

Contributors

Scott D. Appell is the author of the books *Pansies, Lilies, Tulips,* and *Orchids* and editor of the BBG handbooks *Annuals for Every Garden* (2003), *The Potted Garden* (2001), and *Landscaping Indoors* (2000). He lives, writes, and teaches horticulture on Vieques, Puerto Rico; his private consultation company is called the Green Man.

Gwen Barclay and her mother, **Madalene Hill,** are the authors of *Southern Herb Growing* and contributed to the BBG handbook *Gourmet Herbs* (2001). They have also written articles for *The Herb Companion, The Herb Quarterly, Neil Sperry's Gardens, Texas Gardener,* and other publications. Madalene is a past president of the Herb Society of America, and Gwen has chaired both the South Texas and Pioneer units of the society. They were instrumental in forming the Texas Herb Growers and Marketers Association, and Gwen served as its organizational chairman and first president. She is now director of food service for the International Festival-Institute at Round Top, Texas. Madalene developed the McAshan Herb Gardens for the Festival-Institute, where she now serves as curator of the gardens.

Susan Belsinger is a food writer, educator, and photographer based in Brookeville, Maryland. Her work has appeared in *Gourmet, Herb Companion, Kitchen Gardener, Natural Home, Organic Gardening, The Washington Post,* and other publications. Her books include *Basil: An Herb Lover's Guide, The Garlic Book, Flowers in the Kitchen,* and *Herbs in the Kitchen,* and she contributed to the BBG handbooks *Gourmet Vegetables* (2002) and *Gourmet Herbs* (2001).

Claire Hagen Dole is the former publisher of *Butterfly Gardeners' Quarterly* and editor of the BBG handbook *The Butterfly Gardener's Guide* (2003). She writes about wildlife gardening for numerous print publications and for her website, www.butterflygardens.com. She lives in Seattle, Washington.

Donna Gerbosi-DiFulvio is a garden and food writer and photographer specializing in herbs. Her work has appeared in *Newsday, The Herbarist,* and other publications. An instructor at several botanical gardens, she also lectures extensively on herbs, gardening, cooking, food preservation, and plant folklore. She lives on Long Island, New York, and is a past president of the Long Island unit of the Herb Society of America.

Beth Hanson is former managing editor of BBG's gardening handbooks and is editor of six BBG handbooks, including *Spring-Blooming Bulbs* (2002), *Summer-Blooming Bulbs* (2001), *Gourmet Herbs* (2001), *Natural Disease Control* (2000), *Chile Peppers* (1999), and *Easy Compost* (1997). She also contributed to *The Brooklyn Botanic Garden Gardener's Desk Reference* (Henry Holt, 1998). She lives outside New York City and writes about gardening, health, and the environment for various publications.

Deirdre Larkin is a horticulturist and historian with a special interest in the use of historical techniques in restored and re-created gardens. She worked for ten years in the gardens of the Cloisters branch of the Metropolitan Museum, in New York City, where she continues to lecture on plants and gardens in medieval life and art. She is an instructor for the New York Botanical Garden and a consultant on garden projects and programming to the Center for Medieval Studies at Pennsylvania State University. She gardens in upstate New York.

Holly Shimizu is the executive director of the U.S. Botanic Garden in Washington, D.C., and former managing director of the Lewis Ginter Botanical Garden, near Richmond, Virginia. She contributed to the BBG handbook *Gourmet Herbs* (2001), served as editorial consultant on the Eyewitness handbook *Herbs,* and was a coauthor of *The American Garden Guide Book on Herb Gardening.* She was also one of the hosts of the television show *Victory Garden* and developed *Holly Shimizu's Video Guide to Growing and Using Herbs.*

Tina Marie Wilcox has been the head gardener and herbalist at the Ozark Folk Center's Heritage Herb Garden in Mountain View, Arkansas, since 1984. She tends the extensive gardens, plans and coordinates annual herbal events and workshops, and facilitates the production and sale of plants, seeds, and herbal products for the park. She also gives lectures and workshops throughout the United States in herb growing, living history, and herb use.

Illustrations
Steve Buchanan

Photos

Karen Bussolini cover, pages 2 (courtesy of Enfield Shaker Museum), 24, 50, 59, 60

Alan & Linda Detrick pages 4, 28, 55, 104

Jerry Pavia pages 7, 15, 16, 18, 19, 20, 21, 23, 31, 43, 44, 47, 48, 49, 54, 57, 68, 70 both, 76, 80 bottom, 84, 93 both, 94, 96, 106, 107, 108, 109, 111

Walter Chandoha pages 8, 86, 97

Derek Fell pages 10, 62, 82, 94

David Cavagnaro pages 14, 17, 22, 29, 33, 35, 36, 45, 46, 56, 58, 60, 66, 67, 71, 72, 77, 90, 98, 99, 100, 110

Neil Soderstrom pages 30, 32, 69, 83, 91, 95, 112

Gwen Barclay page 34

Susan Belsinger page 37

Elvin McDonald pages 38, 42

Holly Shimizu pages 78, 80 top, 81, 85

Index

More Information on Growing Herbs

Gourmet Herbs: Classic and Unusual Herbs for Your Garden and Table is an indispensable guide for backyard gardeners and gourmet cooks alike. In addition to tips and information about choosing, growing, and harvesting, including a comprehensive encyclopedia of classic and exotic herbs, this guide is full of delicious recipes featuring the bounty of your garden.

Ordering Books From Brooklyn Botanic Garden

World renowned for pioneering gardening information, Brooklyn Botanic Garden's award-winning guides provide practical advice for gardeners in every region of North America.

Join Brooklyn Botanic Garden as an annual Subscriber Member and receive three gardening handbooks, delivered directly to you, each year. Other benefits include free admission to many public gardens across the country, plus three issues of *Plants & Gardens News, Members News,* and our guide to courses and public programs.

For additional information on Brooklyn Botanic Garden, including other membership packages, call 718-623-7210 or visit our web site at www.bbg.org. To order other fine titles published by BBG, call 718-623-7286 or shop in our online store at www.bbg.org/gardengiftshop.